SONIA OVERALL

Sonia Overall is a writer, psychogeographer and writing tutor living in East Kent. Her published work includes novels, poetry, short stories, academic articles and features, many of which touch on psychogeography, spirit of place and aspects of the weird. Sonia is a member of the Walking Artists Network and founder and curator of Women Who Walk, a network for walking academics and creatives. She is currently a Senior Lecturer at Canterbury Christ Church University, where she runs the MA in Creative Writing.

OLIVER BARRETT (ILLUSTRATOR)

Oliver Barrett is a musician and illustrator based in Somerset. He releases music under his own name, Petrels, Sun Do Silver, Glottalstop, Sphagnum Moss, and many more besides. His first, self-illustrated book, *The Nuckelavee*, was published by Tartaruga Press in 2015. You can see more of his work at floatinglimb.com

Heavy Time

A PSYCHOGEOGRAPHER'S PILGRIMAGE

Sonia Overall

with illustrations by Oliver Barrett

Penned in the Margins

LONDON

PUBLISHED BY PENNED IN THE MARGINS
Toynbee Studios, 28 Commercial Street, London E1 6AB
www.pennedinthemargins.co.uk

The right of Sonia Overall to be identified as the author of this work has been asserted by her in accordance with Section 77 of the Copyright, Designs and Patent Act 1988.

First published in 2021

Printed in the United Kingdom by TJ Books Limited

ISBN
978-1-908058-83-6

*In fond memory of Christopher
Cherry: tutor, mentor and friend.*

Heavy Time

The Call

Walsingham

Ely

Southwark

Rochester

Canterbury

N

trinities

ridge   furrow   desire line
ditch   dyke   holy well
leaf   stock   root strike

SOME MORNINGS, YOU STAND IN the shower for as long as you can, savouring the momentary space it gives you. After that, the erosion begins, wiping away all creative thought: the demands and refusals of a child; the clamouring of social media; the screaming headlines of billboards; the slow ratchet of traffic and public transport as you slidewalk to work; the petulant ping of another email skating into your inbox. Then home, the tension of your bow another notch tighter: clothes to wash, meals to cook, errands to run – a multitude of small tasks undone by the hands of others. Reverse the routine: unpeel, reset. Repeat. Your imaginative life is, as Adrienne Rich wrote, 'thought sleeping... certified dead'.

Then an idea comes to you. It comes suddenly, a rare flash in a rarer moment of solitude. You are in the bath. You picture yourself stepping out onto a path like The Fool in the tarot, a bundle on a stick, tripping lightly. You imagine shedding responsibility, stepping off the treadmill, wandering the lanes. But not an idle wandering: this has meaning. It is the recovering of sanity and sanctity. You want to remember what it feels like to have the freedom of ideas, to follow your interests, to scrutinise encounters. To stop the endless chatter and absent yourself from the secular spectacle. You picture yourself on a pilgrimage.

❖

Pilgrimage, according to Pope Benedict XVI, is the stepping away from oneself in order to encounter God. There is something in that. You do not expect to find God; you are an agnostic with animist tendencies. But you do want to find thin places: pockets in the landscape where the membrane is so tightly stretched that other worlds might shine through. You want to see the holy in the everyday – in hedgerows, in the shredded ectoplasm of plastic bags clinging to chain-link fences, in a field of sugar beet.

You might find it if you walk the old pilgrim ways, if you put your feet on the same paths and seek your version of the sacred. You remember a small town near the coast: you were fourteen, fifteen maybe. Little Walsingham. It had a souvenir shop and a shrine, candles and bookmarks and a tearoom. But it also had something else: a stillness like snow, a reverence. You've never forgotten standing in its hushed, narrow streets and feeling your body hum like a plucked string, vibrating from an unseen force. Later, reading about the shrine and the priory, the footfalls of visitors over the centuries, you wondered if it was the press of the past that struck you, the longing of all those people. You regard reliquaries as artefacts – the interest comes in the investment of others. What do you invest in? Place. Walking. Process.

❖

Once upon a time there was a little girl who lived in a place that was very flat. The land stretched out and rolled towards the horizon. The skies were huge. The soil was black.

A river ran through the town where the girl lived. There were ducks and swans on the river, and long, low boats that came and went. Some of these boats were floating houses with gardens on the roofs, flowers in pots and brightly-painted enamel jugs that shone in the sunlight from those big, open skies.

The river called to the girl. She knew that it ran from the town to other places. The water had to start and end somewhere, because it was always moving, even when it seemed still. The girl longed to follow this river; to discover the secret places where it ran; to see its banks and the fields that lay either side; to see how it broke those banks when it grew too large and became greedy, spreading itself out over the black soil and swallowing up the roots of trees.

As she grew up, the girl longed to explore alone beyond the town. She longed to follow that river and wished herself into those black fields, where she might look back at the town and see its towers and the lights in the houses glowing like lanterns in the darkness.

One night, the girl lay awake in her bed. Her brother was asleep. Her parents were asleep. But she could not rest. Something stirred in her that would not be quiet. She sat up in bed and looked at the curtains drawn across the window. She could hear the sounds of the night from behind those curtains: the cry of a creature somewhere in the blackness, the hum of the vast skies. She drew back a curtain and looked into the navy-dark garden below. After a while the shapes of the garden began to form. She could see the trees and the swing, the chicken coop and the tool shed. She wanted to be out there. She wanted to smell the black earth and the apple tree as its leaves breathed into the cool night air. She wanted to feel the damp of the ground climbing, the dew settling around her feet.

She got out of bed, put on her coat and shoes and tiptoed through the house. She opened the garden door. The air was cool and the night called her. The sky was huge and splashed with stars. The moon winked at her from its place above the far fence.

Don't tell, she said to the moon.
Never, the moon replied. This is our secret. Come and see.

So the girl crossed the damp grass to the back fence. She opened the gate and went out towards the moon. The moon nodded in the sky, so she followed it, walking between the quiet houses, past the empty playground, through the streets, into the horizon.

The girl walked until she grew cold and tired and wanted her bed again. She thanked the moon for showing her its secret night-time town and the way that the houses and paths and the long, low horizon all seemed so different.

The girl lay down and went to sleep. In the morning she looked out of her window again and all was back to normal. The only changes were the line in the damp grass where she had walked to and from the gate, and the hem of her nightdress still touched with dew. Nobody else had noticed.

The girl and the moon kept their promise. But the girl's night walk told her something that she had always suspected: she was restless. The horizon and the sky and the river and the fields would keep on calling, and sometimes she would answer them, and leave.

❖

When you grow up in the flatlands, the horizon is always in sight. The edge of the landscape calls to you. Challenges you. Look out of a first-storey window and you can see for miles. Vast black fields of fen soil, edged with the stocky lacework of hedgerows. Dykes and ditches that hold back rising floodwater with their strong-armed banks. Railway sidings and towpaths. Squat church towers nudging the skyline. If you're lucky, a village green, where the genius loci of a yellow-eyed billy goat is tethered to a post.

There is always something out there. Over there. You can almost see it, but it will take you hours to get there. The fen horizon is peripheral, perpetual; the sky is enormous. Walk towards the edge and watch the rotoscope turn. You can lose yourself, but it's hard to get lost. With so much lined up along the edges – farm buildings like ornaments on a shelf – there is always something to steer towards.

❖

Pilgrimage has distinct stages. Like weathered stone or a passage worn by many feet, this form of walking has been shaped and smoothed through time and use. Labels differ according to faith and creed, but the structure is universal.

First, the call: a yearning, a summoning, the catalyst for pilgrimage. Then the stage of preparation: extricating the self from everyday life, making arrangements, seeking permissions. Next, the journey itself, taking in solitude or companionship on the way. At some point on the journey, the pilgrim is immersed in the landscape: no longer a mere observer, they reach a stage of absorption and spiritual contemplation. Arrival is the stage of culmination, the achievement, marked by the ritual of a shrine visit, the lighting of a candle, a chosen intervention. The journey back must follow if the pilgrimage is to be a distinct experience, rather than just part of a greater wandering. Finally there is reintegration, returning to the former life. The result is, ideally, peace, humility and clarity; the healing of ills, the descending of grace, the world seen with fresh eyes.

You have heard the call. You know what you need to do: you are going to walk to Walsingham.

❖

The medieval pilgrim travelled in search of the sacred, but to journey forth was also a symbolic setting-apart of the conventional self, stepping away from the responsibilities and restrictions of the ordinary. I too want to unwind the spool, to disentangle myself from the everyday, to find space and clarity and maybe – maybe – a little chink of faith.

I am not a long-distance walker. I have never climbed a mountain or trekked across a moor. But I'm sturdy, and stubborn, and relentlessly curious about place. My creative life is bound up with walking: walking-writing, psychogeography, the layered sensory experiences of moving through, and dwelling in, different spaces. I walk and write, carrying a notebook, sniffing out settings and stories. I walk to understand characters in fiction, my own and others; to become a character, seeing and reimagining the world and moving through it, one foot in the real and one foot in the fictional, balancing between them or tipping over. I write walking poems, lines created by ambulant observation, the rhythms and shifts of pedestrian movement. I walk streets and country lanes and footpaths, trackways and barrows and standing stones, edgelands and margins and unloved in-betweens, out-of-season resorts and derelict pleasure gardens.

Unlike a medieval pilgrim, I'm not looking for miracles. I am looking for the everyday divine, the gods of hedgerows and laybys. I am on the psychogeographical scent, a hunter of spirits of place. Psychogeography is the study of how place makes us feel and act. It's a loaded term, roots deep in Situationist theory and resistance against consumerism, a rejection of urban monotony and private land ownership. Psychogeography is bound up with the dérive or drift, a practice that encourages the walker to push back against expected ways of moving through public space, following curiosity rather than signage. It's a form of re-enchantment as well as resistance, a playful response to feeling for the unseen signals of place. So far, so good. But as numerous detractors have pointed out, psychogeography is a predominantly white, working class, male affair. It is often seen as an extension of the idle wanderings of the flâneur, a figure that first features in the literature of Edgar Allan Poe, Baudelaire and Walter Benjamin. Observing, strolling, judging: not walking as necessity or expediency, but as an expression of heteropatriarchal privilege. Psychogeography, it would seem, is something men do.

But it isn't. I do it. I know lots of women who do it. And I claim the term for myself: I am a psychogeographer. Why? Because 'psychogeography' does exactly what it says on the tin, intersecting mind and place. Because although I often walk to get from A to B, and do not drive, and although walking for its own sake is a rarity that I must snatch between daily demands and responsibilities, I can still drift, and wander, and resist with my feet if I want to.

At least, I do when I get the chance.

A psychogeographical drift is a time out, a walk that resists notions of busyness or productivity. So does pilgrimage. Both are ways of walking that explore our sense of self: challenging habits, being with our thoughts, rejecting materialism. Both practices seek to connect the walker with the environment in meaningful ways. I want to see if I can bring these methods of walking together. I want to carve out the time to walk to places that are meaningful to me, and to drift a little along the way, embracing serendipity. As a psychogeographer, I want to tune into how the places I encounter affect me, physically and emotionally. As a pilgrim, I hope this tuning-in will lead to a state of immersion and, ultimately, a meaningful arrival. Whatever happens, the journey will give me the time and space to reconnect body, brain and landscape.

❖

Walsingham in Norfolk – specifically the village of Little Walsingham – was one of the most visited sites in medieval Northern Europe. Its Anglo-Saxon shrine was supplemented by a 12th-century priory; as a centre of English medieval pilgrimage, it was second only to Canterbury. In my late teens I moved from Ely in Cambridgeshire to Canterbury to study; stayed, and now work in another university there. As I start to plan my pilgrimage, it strikes me that I have a trinity of places to connect, a triangular journey to make. Canterbury is still on my doorstep. Walsingham is my ultimate goal, and I'd like to get there from Ely, my childhood home, just as I did on that formative visit. Looking at a map, there's a line to be drawn from Canterbury to Ely via London. And so my stations are laid out, my dots to join: Canterbury, London, Ely, Walsingham.

Canterbury is laden with references to Chaucer – a

Chaucer Hospital, a Chaucer School, a Chaucer Care Home – and characters from his *Canterbury Tales* infiltrate business names and pub signs. Chaucer's pilgrims set out from Southwark, travelling from London to Canterbury, and I seize on the possibility of a pleasing reversal: I will walk their route the other way. It's an instant meeting of psychogeographical disruption and linear pilgrimage. Going backwards feels like the right way to begin a journey of experiencing things anew.

Planning the route itself is more complex than I expected. It transpires that there is no single, authentic, documented medieval pilgrim's way between Southwark and Canterbury, and Chaucer's narrator only name-checks a few stops along the journey. However, there's little doubt that pilgrims travelling from London walked or rode along sections of what is now the A2. It's an ancient path, morphing from Celtic trackway to paved Roman road to the Anglo-Saxon Watling Street, built upon and built upon and seeping into parallel bypasses until reaching its current shape, an artery connecting London to Dover and the continent. I've walked alongside busy roads before, but even if I faced down heavy traffic and dodged the attention of transport police, some stretches of the A2 are a no-go for pedestrians.

I look at Ordinance Survey maps and regional walking routes, and order a set of published pilgrimage guides by Rev.

John Merrill, a marathon walker and writer. Merrill's guides are enthusiastic and well-intentioned hybrids, perfect for planning a walking holiday that takes in sacred sites. They are also full of detours that eat up extra days and add on surplus mileage.

I have two weeks to get to Walsingham and back again. Wrestling this much time away from work and home has been a miracle in itself, and I need to make every mile count. I stitch together an itinerary that joins my major sites as directly as possible, based on what knowledge I can glean about likely medieval routes. It's a patchwork of roadsides, footpaths and cycle ways. It dawns on me that the very idea of a set, traditional pilgrimage 'way' is rather bogus: a romantic, post-Enlightenment imposition. Yes, pilgrims would use established paths and roads to cut across the country, but they would also hitch a ride on passing carts, travel by boat and, when weather affected the terrain or roads were especially busy, take minor detours. Interruptions and digressions did not make a pilgrimage any less authentic. Without the infrastructure of medieval wayfaring, with its roadside hostelries and monastic hospitality, my route is also dictated by the logistics of overnight stops. Contemporary pilgrims in organised church groups can get around this by 'champing', glamping in churches and friendly chapels, but I'm obliged to fit my path around cheap motels, Airbnbs and rooms above pubs.

I map out my journey according to the sides of that triangle. Leg one is Canterbury to Southwark via Faversham, Rochester and Greenwich, a journey of roughly seventy miles. From Southwark, I'll head north out of London towards Ely. For me, Ely is going home, back to the place from whence all wanderings began. With no equivalent to Chaucer's route for this section, I'll lay my own desire paths over bits of Merrill's guides, recreational walking routes and country lanes, using Waltham Abbey, another significant pilgrimage site, as a steering point. Leg two is therefore open to improvisation, and I calculate it as around ninety miles. Leg three, Ely to Walsingham, has more established pilgrim stations, if not definite paths. Ely was an island until the Fens were drained in the 17th century, and travel in this area would have required navigating waterways. Crossing the Fens is still tricky on foot, with stretches of walking along high dykes and few footpaths, but once into Norfolk I can tag onto part of the old Peddars Way to Swaffham and Castle Acre. I make that a final shift of fifty or so miles.

Canterbury Cathedral and St Thomas; Ely Cathedral and St Etheldreda; Little Walsingham and Our Lady. Three legs to my journey: three major sites of medieval pilgrimage.

I tear pages out of Merrill's London to Walsingham and Ely to Walsingham guides, retaining the relevant bits. I buy OS

Explorer maps to patch together the gaps, and a map case to keep them dry. I fill, empty and repack my rucksack. I have walking shoes and sensible clothes and a lightweight water bottle. I keep meaning to find time for some warm-up walks, a few practice runs to toughen up my soles and stretch my calf muscles, but with two weeks of leave coming up there's so much to get done. In the final days, it seems selfish to disappear on a walk and leave my family behind; I'll be doing that soon enough. I print out my itinerary with its list of stops and phone numbers and decide that at this point, I'm as ready as I'm going to be. I know where I'm heading, and roughly how I'll get there. I've got places to sleep and a phone for emergencies. What could possibly go wrong?

The Way

mantra   for walking alone

not drawing in the horns   but putting out the feelers

not rootless   but tapping in

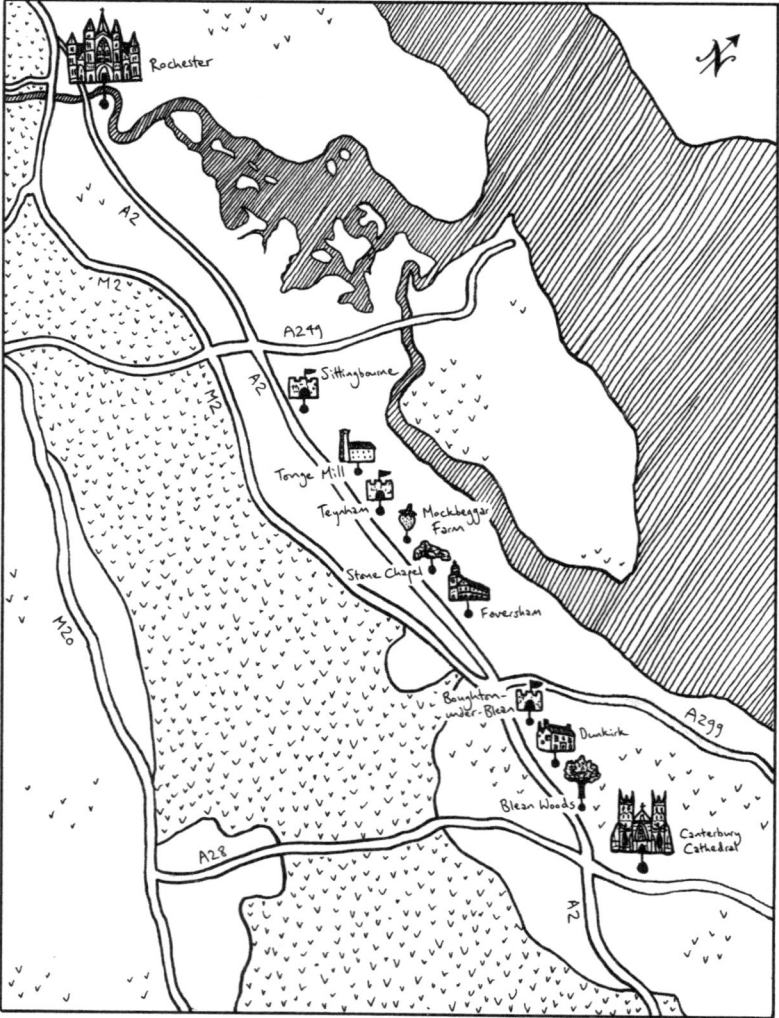

Rochester

A2

M2

A249

Sittingbourne

A2

M2

Tonge Mill

Teynham

Mockbeggar
Farm

Stone Chapel

Faversham

M20

Boughton-
under-Blean

Dunkirk

A299

Blean Woods

Canterbury
Cathedral

A28

A2

To Southwark

THE KING IS BAREHEADED, BAREFOOTED. Dressed in sackcloth. The crowd is restless as he speaks. Several onlookers jeer. When he mentions the name of the archbishop, the jeering swells to a roar. The queen is aloof, contemptuous. A guard raises his polearm and surveys the gathering.

It's the 7th of July. Today, the city of Canterbury commemorates the penitential pilgrimage of Henry II, in July 1174. An actor takes his part, reprising Henry's apology for the murder of his Archbishop, Thomas à Becket. Whatever the truth of the quarrel between king and priest, Becket's assassination – on holy ground, in the sanctity of his own cathedral – is a tale worth retelling. A pageant weaves through the streets: processional giants, musicians, re-enactment militia. Brownie packs and makeshift samba bands. Schoolchildren play the role of chastising Novices, heckling the king and eulogising Becket the martyr. Along the route Henry is ceremonially whipped with ragged streamers, taunted by a white-faced dancer in the guise of Becket's ghost. The sun is blistering.

It's a fitting start to a pilgrimage. I am in this parade, one of the medieval musicians taking the slow walk behind the principal actors. We pause for speeches outside the shopping centre and are chivvied into line by a steward in a hi-vis vest. When we reach the Buttermarket, in the shadow of Christchurch gate, I nip into Yo! Sushi and buy a bottle of water to offer Becket's ghost. This is solid work: measured stepping, walking as if through a treacled wall of heat and bodies, blowing into medieval woodwind. Tarmac and paving stones and cobbles, all tough through the thin soles of re-enactment footwear. It's harder work for Becket in her pancake make-up, slow-leaping in layers of black costume. Our gurdy player retreats into the shaded doorway of a souvenir shop, fanning herself with one hand.

The procession takes a couple of hours altogether. At the end, on the steps of the Marlowe Theatre, there are fanfares, more speeches, some poems. Henry is taken off to be punished by a group of secondary schoolers in hooded robes. The organisers offer votes of thanks; the crowd gradually disperses. One of our drummers emerges from the theatre bar with a tray of beers. I sit in the scant shade by the river and sip mine, knowing that sun and beer and afternoon walking will be a bad combination. Several of the band members are already on duty again, demonstrating medieval crafts, but it's far too hot to light the blacksmith's mobile forge. Punts pass behind the truncated river wall, crouching low in the water. You can often spot eels and trout in the shadow of the bridge here, where the water runs clear and shallow. Not today though. The sunlight falls in white sheets, seeking every surface. Henry II. Thomas à Becket. Christopher Marlowe. Names that will return on this route, to be carried in stages, glimpsed in unexpected places. There will be others too, threads of synchronicity whose stitches will become visible once the walking brain has set in. A little ritual re-enactment is a good place to start, to retrain the mind. A little serious play. One intention of this walk is to see beyond the humdrum marketplace bustle of shops and sights; to experience movement as more than just a body in transit. It will take a while though. Achieving this mindset is, like a shrine to the pilgrim, something to be earned. It probably lies on the far side of exhaustion. How long it will take me to get there? How many days on the road before I begin to open up and feel the cobweb vibrations of place? Will I experience an epiphany? When? Where? I have a long way to walk. What if I'm too numb to feel? What if the body goes into shut down and, with it, the mind? What if all I can manage is to put one foot in front of the other and collapse, wracked, at the end of each day?

My feet are already hot and tired. I eat a late and hurried lunch with my husband and son. We go to the car park and I change out of headscarf, kirtle and shift into peaked cap, shorts and base layer. Bridgedale socks and trail trainers replace medieval slipper shoes. I wriggle into my backpack, adjust the straps. Wriggle some more. We walk together back to the cathedral, pass through the grounds, the scaffolding and hoardings, the site of Becket's shrine. The endpoint of pilgrimage for many; a mid-afternoon start for me. A priest holds his hands above a cluster of people – five men and women with khaki shorts and daypacks – and mutters a blessing. Are they pilgrims, arriving here from Winchester or Southwark? Or are they receiving a blessing for an onward journey, leaving town along the Via Francigena and on to Rome, or across the continent on the Camino de Santiago? Wherever they have been or are going to, they are travelling a good deal lighter than I am.

It's not wise to linger over goodbyes. At the junction of Guildhall Street and the High Street, quaint RAC road signs point each way for the A2: right to Chatham, left to Dover. I promise to keep my mobile phone charged and on, in case I end up in a ditch. A fierce hug from my son, who seems puzzled but proud of his middle-aged mother striding off into the crowd. I turn back to wave. I can't pretend to be doing this anymore. Now I've actually got to do it. My mouth is dry; maybe it's the beer.

Given the city's layout, this part of Chaucer's pilgrims' route is easy to trace: along Canterbury High Street; two bridges over the divided arms of river; past the Pilgrim's hospital with its barrel ceilings and mural traces. THE HOSPITAL OF ST THOMAS THE MARTYR, EASTBRIDGE, lest we forget who died and in what manner. A straight line to the Westgate and on until the London Road, then out, up, away.

Passing under the Westgate means leaving the old city limits, travelling beyond the walls. This is the parish of St Dunstan, another sainted Archbishop of Canterbury. Dunstan once drew the pilgrims here, until Becket supplanted him. The drama of that martyrdom, the skull broken on holy ground, the humbling of a king: Dunstan didn't stand a chance against Becket's story. Like his sainted rival, Dunstan's cathedral tomb was lost to Henry VIII's reformers – there's no trace of it now.

In a vault beneath the floor of St Dunstan's church is another neat echo of Henry VIII's will: the head of Thomas More, 'sometime Lord Chancellor of England'. Removed on Tower Hill on 6th July 1535, displayed on a traitor's pole, More's head was, so the local story goes, retrieved by his daughter Margaret and brought to her husband's manor, here in the parish. Roper Gate, with its heavy wood and decorative stepped brickwork, is all that is left of the Ropers' rich property, The Place. It's an impressive portal of Tudor showiness, stepping skywards and flanked with lozenges. Are there still echoes of horses' hooves here, muffled by this great slab of timber? The gate is a short walk across St Dunstan's Road, opposite the convenience store whose sign screams a misleading FREE CASH above the ATM. The banks along this stretch are long boarded up. Fitness and dance classes are held next door to the lost Tudor manor, but Roper Close and Roper Road give some idea of its sizeable footprint.

July 1174. Back on that summer day, Henry II donned his sackcloth in St Dunstan's church. From there he walked the last humiliating leg of his pilgrimage to Becket's shrine. From the church, it's a left turn onto London Road; undoing Henry's steps, winding back the route.

The end of London Road meets the A2. In the middle of this junction are the Victoria Hotel, a school playing field and a housing estate. I used to live near here, in a poky first floor flat, the place I shared with my husband when we first met. We walked up the footpath to Harbledown many times, foraging on Golden Hill, wallowing in the thought of those Canterbury pilgrims rounding the crest and glimpsing the glittering city below. The route would be easier if I stuck to the road, but it's too tempting: a quick diversion and I can pass the old place again. I give a wave to the windows, send a photo of the building to my husband, continue along the slope. Once, we went this way in search of the old leper hospital of St Nicholas, and found the Black Prince's well. It was a stony niche topped with ivy, a worn step down to the puddle of holy water. A small snake was curled around in the damp space beneath the crowning, carved fleur-de-lys – or at least we said it was a snake. The wyrm of Harbledown. No doubt it was a slow worm darkened by shadow. But the well was real enough: frequented by travellers, pilgrims and those seeking cures for ailments, including the lepers of St Nicholas. Becket and the Black Prince came and drank from here; the Black Prince called for water from this well on his deathbed, but alas, no miracle followed. Becket left a shoe behind for posterity and, once beatified, the name St Thomas's Well began to stick.

I'm off track already. Instead of retracing and walking along the road into Harbledown, I'm up on Golden Hill. I take a desire path through the overgrown grass. The view is more obscured than I remember. Are there more trees? I can't see the way down. I climb back up and scan the horizon. There is the church, and barn roofs, farm buildings. There's no clear path so I make my own, risking nettle stings and bramble backlash. At a gap in the trodden-down fence I stumble out into a field of stubble and rubbish, cross the heavy clods to the back of the farm. The track around the buildings brings me to the village. Lower Harbledown.

If I'm going to get to Faversham I need to stick to the plan: no more diversions. No time to look for the well today – it could be right behind me, but then I could be deceived. My calves sting: the raised bumps of nettle rash are spreading up my left leg and there's a red-pricked scratch below my right knee. I need to be more disciplined: this is not a very clever start.

Palmers Cross Hill feeds into the main road; the heat haze and dust of passing cars is relentless. Looking down from the flyover, the car bonnets shimmer. I can follow a section of smaller Roman Road instead, feeding into Upper Harbledown, but the A2 must be tackled for a stretch before another a string of villages tucks into the crook of it: Dunkirk, Boughton under Blean, Boughton Street. The points on the map are still far enough away to be a distant mirage beyond the roadside.

Now begins my endless noticing of details, a product of extended walking. A running commentary in the head, a procession of images: roadside scrubland and civic shrub planting, passing vehicles, patches of buddleia, dust rising from the giant crushing wheels of lorry cabs, thoughts interrupted by moments of sun-blindness and blaring panels of heat.

This litany is familiar. When I take my notebook for a walk, I'm seeking moments like this. The environment and the rhythm of walking take over. My creative brain is no longer clogged by mundane demands but free to absorb, to turn the glimpsed and ephemeral into a phrase, a fragment, a poem. The heightened noticing that comes from psychogeographical walking is, essentially, a form of wonder. I have a hunch that it's connected to that specific pilgrimage stage of the journey, when the pilgrim reads the signs of the land, seeking wisdom in it. Surely these approaches to walking, and the states they evoke, are connected? If so, I should eventually move on from observation to the stage of immersion. Looking back, will I see this walk as a whole, or only as the sum of its parts? Is a psychogeographical pilgrimage an impossible, two-headed chimera, pulling in different directions? I hope not. I know that once I've covered some distance the noise of noticing and cataloguing will settle down. Perhaps, over time, I will see the bigger picture.

For now, I am happy to dwell in those details. I feel a sudden lightness, a rising elation, a sloughing-off of the everyday. It might not last, but this what I've been aching for: the freedom of stepping out alone and the road to come.

❖

Blean Wood is home to wood ants. Millions of them. Growing up to a centimetre in length, they make vast nests which they thatch with dried grasses and pine needles. Having mild myrmecophobia (a fear of ants), they loom even larger: to me they look like strong-jawed marbles on legs.

Busy in the afternoon sun, the wood ants are a mass of moving pebbles spilling onto the hot tarmac. It's impossible to pause for a moment without the certainty that they will start climbing: shoes, ankles, calves... The only shade to pause in, to stretch for a moment and remove the load, is beneath the trees. Ant territory. Put down the backpack and they are sure to infiltrate, winding their way up the straps and once back on, higher, seeking flesh.

I daren't risk it. I step into the shadow for a moment but the ground is all movement. I snatch up my feet like a gecko on hot sand and retreat back into the heat. The closest I get is to rescue a dark-brown Ringlet butterfly that one ant is trying to carry off, a circus strong-man lifting the sailed wings like a trophy. I pluck the butterfly from its attacker and shake it free. The butterfly staggers on, beats a hard and ragged retreat with its wings; disappears.

Ants: remorseless, single-minded, efficient. Tonight I will dream of a swarm on the carpet of the pub bedroom, an army of squat-legged ball-bearings.

❖

The A2 is a path punctuated by discarded banana peels, mummified by time and weather, curling like the sinister fingers of giant, black leather gloves. I spot many whole gloves too – abandoned gaffer gloves, builders' gloves, rough gardening gloves – in various states of decay. Grey and yellow, rusted or moss-fingered, fraying at the tips and cuffs. They become such a common sight that it's a shock when one glove twitches in the draught of a passing truck – not a glove then, but a flattened pigeon, broken wing-feathers ruffling.

This is the first of the roadkill. Next is a fox, a vivid red and yellow canvas, teeth intact in rictus grin. The brush of its tail is still soft and full of summer colour, dancing in the breeze, waving and lifting like a feathered rush planted in the roadside. Then a whole dappled, rollered rabbit, a perfect two-dimensional specimen that could have been preserved in a flower press. They no longer feel like animals with bones and blood and instincts cut-off by collision; they are cloth, not fur and skin and feathers. Perhaps this is what makes passing them more bearable. Despite the heat, there is no smell.

Aside from the Black Prince's well, the many pilgrim's watering holes along this route have gone. No roadside inns for the thirsty and footsore. But the petrol station is an air-conditioned Aladdin's cave. The man at the counter is glued to the progress of the England match on his propped-up tablet, the small screen angled by the till, feeling for the change for a bottle of Coke rather than looking away for a second. 'England might get through,' he says, 'and reach the semis'. The Coke is ice-cold, sweet, preposterously fizzy and shaken by walking. It is gone in under a minute.

On the road to Faversham I see three lone magpies. According to the rhyme, that's three doses of sorrow. I greet each bird as I see it to undo the spell, and pick up a magpie feather beside the path that edges against Blean woods. This is my first collected object of the walk and the spontaneous beginning of a new ritual for the pilgrimage: selecting and carrying my relic of the day. Later, in the hotel bathroom, I will forget about this feather, wash my shorts in the sink with it still curled inside the buttoned pocket. The feather will be intact in the morning, the quill a curved spine and the blue-black barbs swiftly teased out into a flat paddle again. Like the relics which follow, it will travel all the way with me, and home again.

❖

The Red Lion pub is open but dark inside. Two couples flirt and smoke by the front door. This is the site of another kind of pilgrimage and relic-hunting. In 1838, The Red Lion hosted the body of Sir William Courtenay, a self-styled prophet, Knight of Malta and King of Jerusalem. Courtenay's story is well-known in East Kent: he's a local hero, a mad prophet declaring class truths, a maverick with a made-up name. Courtenay spoke out against the Poor Law Amendment Act and revenue laws as examples of oppression by the rich. He raised a small rebellion in the area, and fell in an armed uprising in the woods near here, just above Dunkirk. *The life and extraordinary adventures of Sir William Courtenay, knight of Malta*, published by James Hunt in the year of Courtenay's death, details this 'Battle of Bossenden Wood'. According to testimony, Courtenay was armed with pistol and bludgeon, and surrounded himself with men, 'with a flag near them in the centre'. Struck down with a sword, Courtenay and his dead followers were laid out on the floor of the Red Lion's stables. Hunt's book includes a plate that depicts them there in the straw, Courtenay in the middle of the diminished corpses 'as a giant among men of moderate size'.

Courtenay's body attracted followers who, believing in his divinity, carried off scraps of his bloodied shirt 'as precious relics to be preserved'. Even though Courtenay was a Cornish impostor in fancy clothes, who had spent time inside the Kent County Lunatic Asylum, there were plenty who wanted to believe in him. A Robin Hood figure with a Messiah complex, he died a few weeks before the coronation of Queen Victoria and the long, grim era of the workhouse. I am tempted to pause here and pay my respects, but there's no 19th-century reliquary to be seen and I must keep going, at least to the next village pub.

❖

Boughton under Blean is a glorious gem after the roadside carnage and drudge of heat. This is biscuit-tin Kent: whitewashed cottages, round-bellied bays and timber-framed jetties. Chaucer's pilgrims take a path through the forest at 'Boghtoun under Blee', marking the start of The Canon's Yeoman's Tale and their final stretch before a first sighting of Canterbury. The road is low and the path raised, with steps down at intervals for crossing sides. Sweet peas bob over squat hedges. Statuesque hollyhocks in macaroon-pastel colours hug the walls.

I succumb to the second pub on the road and order a pint of tonic and soda. The locals in The White Horse are friendly, curious, advising on the route, discussing tactics for crossing the A2 roundabout. The barmaid turns the fan on the counter in my direction; the dried hops above the optics give an autumnal rustle. 'Are you walking for charity?' one man asks. 'No,' I say. 'Just because.' It's easier than attempting to explain. 'Well, bloody good for you,' he says, raising his pint. 'Cheers to that.' Conversation turns to comparing local knowledge of the 'real' Pilgrim's Way, the miles to London and how many steps their digital pedometers have counted that day. I ease off the barstool and shrug back into my pack. There's no need to pee – the heat has evaporated that bottle of Coke. I leave to a cheer and cries of 'good luck!' that give me wings as far as the main road.

When the Boughton Bypass runs out, the roar of the A2 kicks in. To escape a section means a sizeable detour, walking the other three sides of a square around fruit fields. Nine Ash Lane; South Street; Brenley Lane. The roads are narrow but the hedgerows are shady. There are numerous dustbins by the roadside, and a long passing place or layby against Brenley Lane.

It's a curious place for picnickers and rest stops – or are these for the ghosts of pickers and hoppers past to amass in the summer? There's no sign of life today, except the odd passing car, drivers clocking a lone walker with brazen curiosity.

Soon there's no alternative but to join the A2 and cross the roundabout. It's not so tricky after all, the tides of traffic buffered and bunched by lights, cars moving in predictable shoals and easy to manoeuvre through. From here, the long stretch of London Road to Faversham is straight and plodding. The end of the road is almost in sight but there is always another rise, another false turning, another cul-de-sac – until finally, there is the beginning of the town: the Elephant pub, the station road, antique shops and hanging baskets and parked cars, Saturday shoppers back home and the long summer evening still to come.

❖

I cross the railway station platforms and climb out into the mouth of Faversham, the Railway Hotel and rest. As I step inside, the door propped open against the heat, a man with a pint in his hand looks up and winks. 'You look like you've just climbed a mountain,' he says. 'I have reached the top,' I say, and check in at the bar. I would stop for a drink, but I'm too keen to remove my shoes to linger.

I have arrived; the first day of walking is done. So how does it feel? I peel off my socks and examine the state of my feet. Walking, I was constantly aware of the jointed lever of my left foot, lifting and pressing, lifting and pressing. The soles of my feet were fine until that last London Road stretch, but the top of my left ankle hosts a slow-burning fire. It was exhausting. It was hot. But what did I think about? Mostly the route. Not screwing it up. It wasn't mindful: it was too hot to be zen. *How far since the start? How much further to go? Do I need more sunscreen? Why is my left foot a broken hinge?*

In the shower, the aches are expunged and there is more room for clarity. I think back over the points of my walk so far, my own secular, niggling Stations of the Cross. An initial awareness of the backpack with its straps and pressure points, but this soon passed. The first digression on Golden Hill was a genuine dérive, a compulsion to follow my curiosity. The second was a wrong turn that meant tracking back and forth along a section above the A2 looking for a way down. It was a frustration rather than a chance to explore, and it added extra mileage. Despite the minor irritations, there was also that first hour of excitement, the sudden swoop of joy at everything yet to come. And finally, when the end was almost in sight, everything just hurt.

I am reminded of that second stage of pilgrimage: preparation. Mine has been scant. Yes, I checked routes, bought some kit and stocked up on blister plasters. But I have not trained. My body is sluggish and desk-weary. I have the innate stamina of the dogged and headstrong, but I am unfit. The route today felt steeper at times than the 'mostly flat' suggested by the maps and guides.

Walking today, the same questions rose up from the road. How am I going to cope? How will I do this again tomorrow? And how did those ants get so big?

A change of clothes. Campari soda and bruschetta in the garden of a pizza restaurant, notebook at elbow, surrounded by couples as night falls and the fairy solar lights glimmer into being. There are twenty miles to cover tomorrow; forecasts warn of another spike in the heatwave.

Canterbury feels a lot further away than it is.

❖

Today was always going to be the challenge, the part where it could go wrong. Only the second day of walking, so many more miles to cover, temperatures tipping 30C. Feet already throbbing. Leaving the pub, it feels like I'm stepping out over a precipice:

trusting that my body won't let me down, that I won't lose my way, that I will make it to Rochester unscathed, pride intact.

I'm out of the door by eight, but the empty morning streets are confounding. Maze-like. I know where I need to be – back on the London Road – but I cannot find it. I felt my way here last night, so how did everything get so turned around? I wander up and down side streets that feel as if they should take me there, but curve suddenly, or run out on me. I've ended up on the wrong side of the station, tangled in a quad of streets named like a set of school house teams: Briton Road, Norman Road, Saxon Road, Roman Road. Not the Roman Road that I need to get me out of town.

I stare at the map: my brain processes nothing. Is this just morning stupidity, or have a reached a level of obtuseness that will dog me for the rest of the walk? I stop and tune in to the frequency of the main road, to the rumble of early traffic. Something massive – a tractor? a combine? – is audible under the birdsong and dog barks of residential Faversham. I point myself towards it and come out between houses to find a ride-on mower cutting its way across a swathe of green.

By the time I get to the A2 again, via Canute Road, I've lost half an hour and added needless mileage. It's not a good start. I'm also planning to take another detour soon, to a ruined chapel just outside town. I take off my long-sleeved over-shirt: it's already getting warm.

❖

The Chapel of Our Lady of Elverton, or the Faversham Stone Chapel, or Stone-next-Faversham, is a mile or so from the edge of town. I spotted it on the map when checking the route and, given what I could find of its layered history, it is well worth taking a look as I pass. As a medieval church, this would have made a useful wayside chapel for pilgrims, a pause on the stretch to Canterbury. Abandoned during the Reformation, the chapel is now a footprint of stones in a field, protected by English Heritage. Beneath the chapel, or rather, built into its fabric, is a much older site.

This area was once Durolevum, a Romano-British settlement on a busy paved road, a pause on the stretch between Durovernum (Canterbury) and Durobrivae (Rochester). There was a Roman building here; possibly a mausoleum, possibly a temple. There may have been a timber Saxon church.

The ruins of the chapel are easily missed: a field of bronzed oilseed rape, a cluster of trees, a tiny mown path from the roadside. From a distance, the chapel is an inconsequential-looking pile of rubble, half-hidden by the overhanging foliage of a copse. Greenery has undone this place, yet it somehow keeps it together, binding stone, root and creeping vine.

The sun is warm now, the road beginning to haze. Stepping onto the chapel path into waist-high crop, I'm struck by how painterly and pastoral, how ludicrously picturesque, this setting is. The chapel and copse have become one, standing in the centre of the field, melding into the landscape decade upon decade, century upon century. A crimp in the plain. The crop waves and shushes. The Sunday morning sounds of the road fall away. I laugh, because it's as if someone has asked me to describe the kind of place I hoped to find on this walk, and I have written this, with all its layered romance, into being. I'm still smiling a dozen or so steps in when something else happens.

I've had this feeling many times. There is a coldness around my ankles. It's as if I've stepped into a flooded cellar, or into very deep mud. My feet are not wet – it's not that. There is a weight – like water, like sludge, like gripping hands – pulling me deeper. A dragging in the lower abdomen. The ground is not quite where it ought to be. Stepping again means picking my knees up, navigating viscous terrain.

There's no obvious external change, of course. The mown path is dry crop stubble. The soil is dusty. My shoes are still clean

– nothing has attached itself. But it is undeniable. I feel sick and shaky. I am thoroughly spooked.

It seems foolish to stop. I eye the trees, the silent shapes of corvids rising and falling like bats. The flint walls huddle in the shadow. I am close; almost too close. I shake myself and take another step. The ground tugs harder. My tongue feels huge in my mouth. I am feeling for something out of the corner of my eyes, my ears open to every crackle of crop stem. A wary animal sensing the presence of an unseen other.

It doesn't want me here. I back away, keeping the trees in sight, feeling my way to the field margin.

I put down my pack. Look away towards the road; look back. It's Tolkienesque: that waving crop, the bunch of the copse. Or a film location for some lurid folk horror: the abandoned chapel. Rituals by moonlight. Masked vigils in a Ben Wheatley movie waiting to be made. It's a spot for Arthur Machen to site a weird tale: the walker stumbling upon some otherworldly gathering as he takes a shortcut across the field; years falling away, a covert glimpse across ages. Is that why I'm afraid? Have I just watched too many Tigon films, read too many spooky stories?

The hairs on my arms are standing, cartoon-like, to attention. But this isn't simple fear, not the fight-or-flight of facing a predator. There is something here that I do not want to disturb. I cannot bring myself to follow the crop-cut channel to the walls themselves. It is not just the chapel: it is the melding of stone and soil and trees, of use and misuse, of custom and care and dereliction. It awes, refuses trespass. It feels sacred and, frankly, terrifying.

I've found it already: a thin space, an in-between-worlds place, more than the sum of its parts.

There is a moment before sleep where vision and imagination begin to tunnel, as if the mind is zooming to a distant point. Tipping over. The thread connecting mind and body stretches like the string on a rising balloon. Sometimes that zooming begins to spin: the slow-bobbing spin of a playground roundabout, a vortex into the space of dreaming. There's something of that hypnagogic vortex here. I can see across the field and into the trees, see the veins on the leaves of the trees and the pattern they cast on the flints below, my thoughts telescoping out across the distance and into the far rippling space. But the rest is on the other side of dreaming, and I do not want to go there. Not now. Not alone.

Another time, I tell myself. On this midsummer morning it seems wrong, sacrilegious, to intrude any further.

Foreboding and longing. A still point in the thoroughfare. Perhaps I simply have not earned it yet. Perhaps it is just too soon.

I've got another thirteen days in which to find this. Why here, less than an hour's train ride from my door?

I skirt along the foot of the field, following the main road, then trace the lower corner and edge along Four Oaks Road. The height of the crop masks the chapel walls from this side, the copse troubling but safely distant. I gather a single thin finger of seed from the starry crop as my relic of the day. The field is honey-warm and at peace, the A2 slowly humming into life. I keep watching those treetops until the road snakes me away, out of sight.

Away from the main road, the landscape shifts another gear into bucolic. The A2 becomes a distant tidal wash, a far shore on the horizon. It is possible to navigate a parallel route by keeping it just within hearing to the right, the occasional glimpse of a lorry, metallic in the sunlight, like spotting a whale at sea.

The door of a white cottage is canopied with rambling roses and a pair of Green Man reliefs. Buckland is high hedgerows, undulating fields and scattered farms. By Mockbeggar Farm, a rusted winch hangs intact on the side of a Victorian barn, ancient farm machinery recumbent in the long grass. The etymology of Mockbeggar intrigues me, and when I look it up later, it still rings true: a derelict building, or a site that appears grander than it is, raising and thwarting the hopes of beggars.

❖

The path merges with the village of Teynham, a long straight street, a residential rash in the countryside, and at the outskirts by a junction there is another roadside shrine. A poem, a photograph, some artificial flowers. A wheel attached to the lamppost. Plastic toy motorbikes are glued to the street name in memoriam. Not as permanent as a parting stone or memorial cross, but this site is weathered; the elegy has endured. No council officials have gathered up these tokens to the dead. Those flowers will not rot. Do the family and friends of this lost loved one gather here in anniversary vigils? Perhaps. *Remember, stranger, as you pass by.* There seem to be so many of these spots on country roads now: teenage car crash victims, speeding motorcyclists. The unwary and unprepared. It is hard to imagine living in proximity to such a site without feeling that prick of loss with every passing. But perhaps this is a healthy thing, like the family mausoleum or burial mound: on the edge of the village, on the boundary of the living, but not too remote. Just there, hovering on the periphery. Onwards. Sweating uphill Sunday cyclists nod and smile in shared endurance. Embracing and reclaiming early morning country lanes, they are astir and abroad before the cottage dwellers have started their weekend rounds of grass-cutting, hedge-trimming and barbecue-lighting.

❖

Cows recline beneath an ash in the foreground of Tonge mill and castle, a perfect composition for Sidney Cooper or Constable. The castle is now no more than moat and millpond, but here, where the earthworks can still be traced, was a site of Saxon power play. According to Edward Hasted's *History and Topographical Survey of the County of Kent*, Tonge was created by the wily Saxon chief Hengist. After helping Vortigern, king of the Britons, to defeat the Scots and Picts at Stamford, Hengist claimed his modest reward. He asked for:

only as much land as on ox-hide could encompass; which being readily granted, he cut the whole hide into small thongs, and inclosed within them a space of ground, large enough to contain a castle, which he accordingly built on it, and named it from thence *Thwang-ceastre*, i.e. Thong-castle; whence the parish itself afterwards took its name.

The same legend is attached to other sites in the kingdom, and Hasted points out that the story itself is an imitation of Virgil's account of the building of Carthage. But the tale has stuck, with local variations: sometimes the cunning hero of the ox hide is a local boy putting one over on the landowner.

Tonge's glory now is a 19th-century mill house, the flat millpond fringed with reeds and bobbing mallard ducks, the tapering spindle of brick chimney. Was it here that Hengist made his home? Was this the site where, inviting Vortigern and his nobles to the castle, Hengist's men massacred all but the king? Was it, feasting here, that Vortigern first saw Hengist's daughter Rowena, and threw over his queen to marry the Saxon girl? Hasted's record is begrudging. But maybe; maybe it was here, in this sleepy hamlet near the Swale. Just where that cow is flicking her tail: that's where Rowena stood, holding up a cup of wine to the smitten king. It certainly feels possible this morning.

Dave Tonge, a professional storyteller known as the Yarnsmith of Norwich, has been an acquaintance of ours for many years. The last time he came to Kent and stayed with us, he told us of the Tonge legend, and set out after breakfast to revisit the remains of his family seat. There wasn't much to it, he reported later, and no claim that he can make as lord of the manor. But the fabric of the tale doesn't get any thinner.

Hedgerows, apple orchards, banks of rabbit warrens. This is a landscape to provoke Vaughan Williams or Cecil Sharp; *as I walked out one midsummer morning / for to view the fields and take the air.* Instead, my internal soundtrack is a repeating loop of Clash City Rockers, Staying Alive and a percussively creaking backpack. As I push on, leaving Hengist's home behind, I attempt to strut, pushing up on the balls of my feet to alleviate the rasping in my left ankle. Rooks in the stubble meadow on the route to Bapchild watch me with passing interest, stalking back and forth along invisible lines, tugging at the stubborn ground.

From here, it's back to the shimmering heat of the A2.

Soon I am sunblind from the straightness of it: the relentless forward motion of scowling or blank-faced motorists framed in rectangles of tinted glass. The glare of red, silver and grey car bonnets. It's a painful stretch of the London road: a narrow path, the brown-brick monotony of residential areas, the odd corner shop and crossing place the only landmarks of my progress.

Walking through the pain is possible. The blisters on the soles of my feet mean that I'm stepping onto small, glowing embers. Someone has taken wire cutters to the broken hinge of my left foot, snipping at the tendon cables: when they finally snap at a raised kerb, relief swells. But the heat is impossible: the heat that is building in ferocity, making my head swim.

❖

The edge of the next town signals the beginning of weather over will. My feet are burning intensely now; steps on a griddle. The giddy sickness in my head and throat herald sunstroke. I've been wearing my cap, but the lack of shade has proved too much. I need to stop, to hydrate, to get out of the sun.

I find a café and drink a pint of orange juice. My late-morning veggie breakfast arrives with two rashers of pink and yellow bacon, turning the stomach. Families take up the other tables; a dad studies me with suspicious sidelong glances as he slaps the base of a brown sauce bottle. A yellow-haired girl in a pink halter dress stares, open-mouthed. There is the scraping of knives against toast, the sharp correcting of table manners, the rustling of a newspaper. I stare at the egg yolk congealing on my plate and feel the hot pricking of disappointment behind my eyes. I feel dreadful: nauseous, head thumping, sweat-soaked, raw. The radio is on; the weather report warns against the overheating of dogs and a high pollen count.

I look at my map and my stomach tilts again. Rochester is just too far, too far. I can't do it. I've barely scratched the surface of today's twenty miles and already, I'm beaten: by the sun, by my backpack, by my feeble, blistering feet. To take any distance off the route means walking ten miles along the A2. I picture the hobbling roadside surface, the dust and car fumes, the blanket heat. Beyond that, guaranteed sunstroke and sickness. If I'm not careful now I won't be fit to walk tomorrow. I'm hopeless. I'm a wreck. But I'm not turning back.

It hurts to do it, but I decide to take the train. As I heave myself from the table and stagger into the street, backpack straining my shoulders, it feels like a genuine defeat. But is it really? Perhaps I need to see it as a catapult, a psychogeographical propulsion over distances. Would a medieval pilgrim have turned down a lift when it was offered?

The skin on my soles sears with the pressure of each step. I walk on the outer edges of my shoes, titling my ankles. The long hot stretch of town: the railway station, the road before it broken by square-toothed bulldozers, tarmac crusts oozing wetly in the sun. Will these diggers one day evoke the same nostalgia as this morning's rusted winch and decrepit farm machinery? Halted in this still Sunday air, flies in amber, there is already something antique about them.

❖

The short train journey passes in an insensate fog. At least there is Rochester at the end of it all, Watling Street's bridge over the Medway. The train tannoy bings and announces our arrival. I watch through the window as we edge towards it: not the unfolding of sites that I had imagined, but a panorama through smeared, heat-sticky glass. Rochester: a Norman stronghold, a medieval city of almshouses, a sanctuary for poor travellers.

Rochester cathedral has its own Pilgrims' Steps, to the shrine of St William of Perth, the stone treads worn smooth by visitors and now covered with wood. William was a pilgrim himself, en route to Canterbury, when he was robbed and murdered by his adopted son. When William's corpse appeared to perform miracles he was deemed a martyr. The monks of Rochester brought his body to rest in the cathedral, where it attracted increasing swarms of visitors. The shrine is gone now, of course, lost like Becket's and Dunstan's. I would like to see the steps; the thought of them puts me in mind of Arthur Machen again. In *A London Adventure*, Machen refers to an old worn doorstep as a memorial object. What memories there must be, locked in the stone of those pilgrim steps. As I haul myself upright and shuffle to the carriage door, I resign myself: I'm not going to manage a cathedral tour today.

Rochester is one long main street, a thoroughfare of commerce and architectural gems and jostling Dickensian heritage. The castle with its square sandcastle keep, built by another William, archbishop of Canterbury; before that, a castle by Bishop Odo, a post-conquest show of strength. A sprawling secondhand bookstore ranging over several storeys, proclaiming itself as the largest in the country. I'm glad to be here at last. It seems at last, but is it earned? The hotel reception is empty and the bell brings no response, so I go back into the street, purchase a litre of water and some fruit, seek out a shady seat. Afternoon jazz drifts through the windows of a pub, a dark cavern in the teeth of the sun. It's tempting, but there are no chairs to collapse into, no stools to lean against.

Pilgrim's passages, secret side-alleys, boutiques and restaurants and charity shops. The high street throngs with

T-shirted families and flip-flopped couples displaying designer tattoos and gym muscles, all soaking it up. There isn't a patch of shade to be found that isn't already spoken for by buskers, hawkers, café tables. I pause to read a sign above a tall building, which proves to be an almshouse-turned-museum. A local benefactor Richard Watts left a legacy here, in 1579, to pay for free lodgings for travellers. His promised offering is one night's 'lodging, food, entertainment and four pence' for up to six poor travellers who are not 'rogues or proctors'. If no one appears at my hotel, I might be back to hold him to that. I wander through the crowd and the smell of barbecue, hobble into the hotel reception and ring, ring, ring the bell.

My room is up two flights of creaking floors in the Royal Victoria and Bull hotel. The building boasts a Dickens connection too: a coaching inn that must once have been grand, now a touch decrepit and knock-kneed, bent-backed, moth-eaten. Too large to refurbish, perhaps, and still turn a profit. But there is shade, a fan, water to wash feet. It may look like the bedroom of a slightly impoverished maiden aunt, unloved and untouched since the early 1980s, but following this journey it is a piece of paradise.

After a shower in the beige bathroom, I spread out damply on the bed. From the windowsill pigeons land and lift, land and lift, wing feathers making that percussive, guiro sound, a flamenco

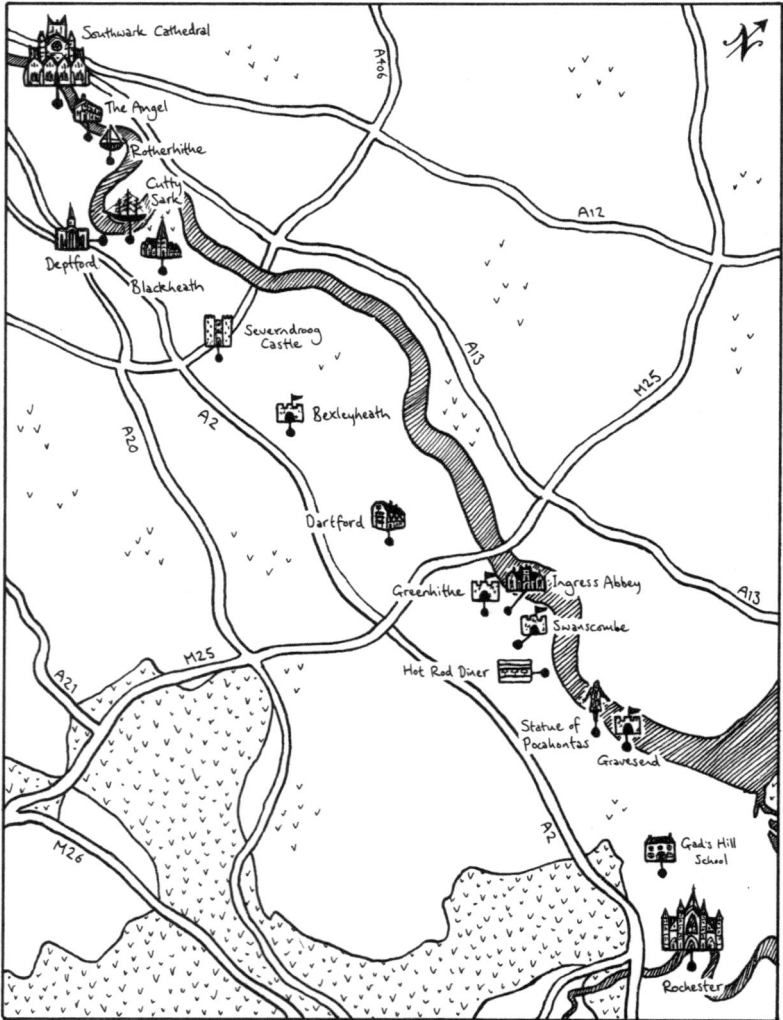

Southwark Cathedral
The Angel
Rotherhithe
Cutty Sark
Deptford
Blackheath
Severndroog Castle
Bexleyheath
A2
A20
Dartford
A406
A12
A13
M25
Greenhithe
Ingress Abbey
Swanscombe
Hot Rod Diner
Statue of Pocahontas
Gravesend
A13
M25
A21
M26
A2
Gad's Hill School
Rochester

fan snapping open and shut. I prop my feet up with a spare pillow. I don't sleep, but my brain drifts wordlessly, as if in a mild fever, images of moving tarmac crowding whether my eyes are open or not. When I look at the time, an hour has passed.

I should explore, find another drink. I force on a pair of plastic sandals. The largest blister amongst a cluster of satellites bursts, flooding the toes of my right foot. There is joy in this weeping: I can walk again. For now.

❖

Rochester Bridge has its own trust, dedicated to maintaining the structure and its heritage. The bridge itself is clearly a matter of civic pride in ornament and engineering: the coats of arms are mirror-bright, scarlet and gold; the recumbent lions and snarling heads are suitably majestic. The bridge has a chapel, discrete but stately with its stained-glass window and curlicued gate, nestled in the Esplanade next to a chunk of ruined town wall. Built in the 1390s, the site was created for travellers and pilgrims to pray for safe passage; upkeep of chapel bridges and other pilgrim conveniences was a common charitable bequest, paving the way from limbo to heaven. This example is one of only a handful left in the country, extensively refurbished and rarely open to visitors.

The Rochester Bridge Trust website explains the presence of medieval bridge chapels by likening them to the airport chapels of today. We may appear to trust jet-propelled engines to prevent us falling from the sky, or the goodwill of our fellow travellers not to rob and murder us in our sleep, but it doesn't hurt to get God on side as well. I check the chapel gate just in case, but I'm out of luck: no quick roadside blessing for my onward journey this morning.

Day three of walking. Crossing the river is taking a deep breath. This is an onward plunge, a stage closer to London. The coast feels far behind now, the tang of the River Medway carrying with it the scent of industry. On the far side is the tangle of Strood, now a vague conurbation; Frindsbury, Downside, the Rede Common Nature Reserve, Broomhill Park. Supermarkets and marina-snug yachts and a garden shed 'showground'. At the slight kink of the river, almost opposite the bridge chapel, is the secret gem of Temple Manor, a 13th-century Knights Templar building. You would never know it was there amongst the warehouses and parked lorries of Knight Road, lying low between the postal sorting office and Morrison's petrol station.

There's no time to visit Temple Manor today, to peer through the green railings at the patchwork of stone and timber, Tudor brick, gothic arches and lattice windows. I've seen it before though, by candlelight, the setting of a one-night-only midwinter performance. The play was an adaptation of a local Becket legend, a site-specific blend of mumming and pantomime. My husband made headdresses and props and performed some puppetry. The whole event was deliberately mysterious. My son (then six) and I arrived at Strood railway station on the night of the winter solstice, where we were greeted by stewards with lanterns who led us in silence through the dark industrial wasteland to the manor. Alight with torches, musicians playing on the steps, my husband with a jig doll dancing on a board, we could have stepped back centuries. We stood around, muffled in scarves and hats, stamping our feet on the frost, grinning from ear to ear. At the end of the evening, cakes and ale went round to celebrate the show and mark the fiddle player's birthday: Ian Cutler, whose youthful playing I had so often admired on *The Wicker Man* soundtrack, was sixty-two. Along with the horses' heads and magic emblems and festive misrule, a treasured sideways glimpse at a folk horror icon for trainspotters like me.

Strood's Becket tale – like the origins of Tonge – has been tweaked by time and telling, but the essence is clear. An altarpiece by the Gothic painter Master Francke illustrates the legend, and it's this image, and variants of it, that any research into the legend will turn up. Becket, riding through Strood on his way to Canterbury, is mobbed by locals, who consider him an enemy of the king. To humiliate him, they cut off the tail of his horse. In the altarpiece painting, the white horse bows its neck, blood staining and streaming from the stump. The culprit holds the docked tail in provocation; a haloed Becket turns back with a benevolent gesture.

In the legend, Becket isn't so saintly or sanguine: enraged, he curses the people of Kent, claiming that they will for ever after be born with tails. In some versions, they sprout tails there and then; in others, their descendants are born with tails, a curse to shame future generations. It's a good story, and one that speaks not only of a local, but a national comeuppance. According to Jan Bondeson in *A Cabinet of Medical Curiosities*, talk of these tails was widely supposed to be true. 'The epithet "Kentish Long-tails" was commonly used well into the 19th century… During the Middle Ages, other countries commonly used the epithet caudatus [tailed] to deride the English.' In his *Perambulation of Kent*, William Lambarde cites the tail legend as an example of European mockery levelled at the English: 'Behold heere one of the fruites of their spitefull miracles'. Tails or no, we continue to cut a poor show on the world stage. We don't need saints to curse us; we are perfectly capable of making ourselves ridiculous.

No more A2 for a while: today I am following the A226

just beyond Rochester, the long Gravesend Road. This is the kind of roadside walking that also involves country hedgerows, with the attendant perils of both. Stingers stretch across the narrow path, seeking elbows. The brambles are strong enough to reach out and lift the hat from my head. Even the mallows with their beguiling purple-and pink-veined trumpets are desiccated and sharp-stemmed. A dry leaf of sycamore falls, barbed and brittle, like an arrow to the neck.

Escaping the salvo of foliage means crossing to the other side of the parallel cycle track, where rat-tail plantain waits to whip at my ankles. It's only just after nine o'clock and hot, hot, hot. The way is uphill.

❖

This is Dickens country: Higham, Gads Hill. At the top of the climb, opposite the Falstaff pub, is an old water trough. I pause to catch my breath and read the plaque set into the ground beside it. This is the old Higham Horse Trough, restored in 1996 by the borough council, parish church and Dickens Country Protection Society. The connection between Victorian literature and this rough slab of container isn't immediately apparent: the trough is as parched as the grass around it, housing only dried-out leaves, a few handfuls of silt and a discarded popsicle sheath. It's a good place to stop though, to stretch the calves and take a swig from the water bottle. Beside the trough is a faceless milestone, one of many I will notice on this route, worn by weather until place names and distances are rendered illegible, like chisel-wrecked faces in a post-reformation chapel.

Rest time is over. Beside the road is a sign advertising Gad's Hill School: a private institution of burgundy blazers and, of course, Dickensian heritage. Suddenly the horse trough makes sense. This is the site of Dickens' country house, Gads Hill Place. He received numerous literary visitors here. He also had that space all writers covet: the writer's hut, a space apart, sacred to the craft. Dickens wrote *Great Expectations* in his Swiss Chalet in the garden. The chalet was relocated to the grounds of Eastgate House, back in Rochester: you can just make out the ornamental bargeboards peeking above the High Street. But here, where the children study algebra or pass notes about the teacher or stare out of the window at the lawn, Dickens fantasised about prison hulks in the Thames Estuary, to the north, beyond the marshes.

The street names I pass have begun to speak of my needs. Water Lane. Crutches Lane. Where is Oasis-serving-espresso-in-the-shade Lane? The stretch between Higham and Shorne offers the first glimpse of a wide, distant river: the Thames. I stop to process this for a moment, perching on the edge of a bench, keeping my backpack on to remind me that this isn't a real stop. On the ground beside the bench I find my relic of the day: a paper Bingo card with words instead of numbers. *Whim. Whoop. Wharf* and *whisper*. It's a game to play against the sounds of roadside walking, the whoosh, whine and whistle of passing vehicles.

I hoist myself up and keep going. The bank is a tangle of flowering old man's beard, hawthorn, MacDonalds wrappers and flattened plastic bottles. A little further on, the 'Roadside Nature Reserve', just beyond the Thames View Crematorium, hosts flowering sweet-pea-like vetch and the bunched daisy-heads of yarrow, populated by hoverflies. Scraps of torn paper dance in the slipstream of passing cars, lifting and falling false butterflies.

Like the small whites that join them, these paper flutterers have charcoal patches on their wings, the remnants of printed German text. A car manual, perhaps? A single grey-and-white trainer, left foot, nestles into the grass, the loose laces embracing the stalks of timothy-grass.

I'm walking like I mean it. The temperature is bearable, I'm getting used to the backpack and it feels like I'm actually making progress, with miles under my belt before breakfast. The parishes of Chalk and Denton blend in a long parade of houses, chip shops and estate agents that line the road to Gravesend. The brain begins to detune, the antennae dull. It's the point when unlikely treasures tend to reveal themselves.

❖

As if on cue, the squat gem of St Mary's Catholic Church in Denton appears between the terraced council houses and new builds, behind the HONEST LABOUR TRANSPORT flatbed trailer. The entrance to the church is a Halloween jack o'lantern, the two long-eyed windows either side of the gaping door stretched in cartoon surprise. Is the church shocked by the volume of oncoming traffic? Or has it heard some terrible tale of what befalls the traveller on this road? Denton blends into Milton Road, the seat of Gravesend, an unprepossessing mile of obstacles: wheelie bins fetid from a weekend of sun, pushchairs parked at the base of steps, fag ends curling like pinkie-toes on the kerbs. A black-and-white cat, young enough to have kitten eyes, scavenges a small mountain of rubbish behind a low wall. Chicken takeaway grease and a lick of ice cream carton amongst the Stella cans. The landscape is merging: I wonder if I'm starting to merge with it. Then there is Gravesend.

❖

The Riverside Leisure Centre offers a green space to recoup. There's bound to be a café here, along the riverfront. Scattered like the leavings of a film shoot around the park are the remnants of New Tavern Fort, a military fortification on the Thames. An 18th-century defence post against the newly rebellious Americas and their allies; a Napoleonic fort; a WWII stronghold. It's a psychogeographer's paradise, blending landscaped pleasure park, riverside strolls, ramparts and emplacements. An artillery store advertises itself with CARTRIDGE SERVING ROOM above a barred door. A raised gunning station offers a clear line of fire at the open air gym, where a trim Australian woman and a large man in a tatty suit grunt and heave at equipment. The Milton Chantry is a chapel-turned-tavern-turned barracks, a medieval hermit crab in an 18th-century brick shell.

I eat breakfast at a vinyl café table. Outside the windows to the right, this stretch of river is a meeting of waterborne industry and the easy promise of leisure. Londoners flocked here to walk the promenade and enjoy the racy pleasures of the pier, until the railway came, with its lure of cheap seaside visits. A young family stops for swings and ice cream; to the left, the funfair has come to town, trailers and vans pulling up on site, ready to metamorphose this patch of grass into an ephemeral festival.

I feel as if I've done well this morning, as if I'm getting into my stride. According to my plan and maps, there are sixteen miles to cover today. I'm getting there, but I need to keep moving. I take the path alongside the river as far as I can before veering into town for supplies.

The local heritage trail points to the Pocahontas statue, standing in the grounds of St George's Church. Pocahontas, Rebecca, Powhatan 'princess'; diplomat, noble savage, social curiosity. What she really was, and what she made of the court of James I, remains unsaid. Her story has been romanticised with retellings, from a verse in Peggy's Lee's 'Fever' to a Disney cartoon. She fell sick at sea, died in Gravesend and is buried somewhere in this earth. This humid July lunch hour, a man sits at her bronze feet, swigging from a giant caffeinated can of Monster. It's not a place to linger.

After a top-up of blister plasters and icy bottled water from the shopping centre, I'm back onto the London Road towards Northfleet. The route is a long straight track now, heat haze on the road, glimpses of docks between high buildings. The services along this stretch have shifted too, inching towards the cosmopolitan: Western Union signs between the nail bars and discount off licenses, calabash amongst the porch-front produce of a convenience store. The bastion of Our Lady of Assumption strides the right bank, its tower like a limb of Battersea Power Station, built to fend off the hordes or cower the locals.

❖

The stretch of roadside linking Northfleet to Swanscombe passes in a muddle of brick and concrete. The sign for the Cement Industry Heritage Centre seems to point to a nearby block of flats. A shattered plastic knife on the ground has taken the shape of a perfect miniature cutlass. The heat is now ferocious. A single-toothed old woman sits on a stool in the centre of her barren front garden, yellow grass and paving slabs, a triangle of shade from the house. She smiles and puffs her cheeks at the sky.

Hot Rod Diner offers incongruous cream-and-chrome luxury opposite the housing estate. *Come in to the cool*, the shades say. The piped rock-and-roll is a siren call: there will be air conditioning, padded leatherette booths, soda floats. It is almost time to stop, but today's holy grail is a pub in Swanscombe, where a cold beer will be well deserved: keep going. Keep going.

❖

Except that the pub is closed. There are seats outside, but not an inch of shade. Traffic idles at the crossroad lights a few feet away. Double-deckers sigh exhaust fumes. Roadworks on the High Street drill and thrum. Today smells of hot tarmac, dust and diesel. If only the trees were in blossom: there was the odd hanging basket and window box outside the pubs of Northfleet, but none of those petunia-laden offerings were close enough or likely to scent.

A fingerpost points at a footpath to the river. There may be shade down there; perhaps a café. I follow the path, which soon reveals itself as typical urban edgeland, a margin of neglect between the used car lot and industrial units. Discarded sandwich wrappers and broken office furniture poke through the buddleia and nettles. 'Danger Deep Excavation' signs and concrete bollards.

CCTV cameras and security dog warnings. It's even less hospitable than the town, so I retrace my steps, back to the nudging traffic, the hammering on tarmac and pavement closures. A truck swings to skirt around the diversion sign, narrowly missing a woman with a double buggy. Pedestrians hang back on the narrow strip of path by the railway, waiting for a gap to cross in. At least the Co-op is open and the ice-cream freezer still stocked. I attempt to eat an orange iced-lolly faster than it melts, risking wasp-and-fly-trap dribbles on chin and T-shirt. The pub is still closed, so I launch a double-attack, alternately ringing the bell and phoning contact numbers until a man in a grubby white vest, spanner in hand, lets me in. I throw down my pack, ease off my shoes and make the most of my afternoon timing with a long, cool shower in the shared bathroom.

The room above the pub is clean and compact, but stuffy in the hanging heat. By seven o'clock, the prospect of staying put throughout the long summer evening depresses. I don't want company, but I do need air. I go downstairs to the bar with my notebooks and the map for tomorrow's route. There's no beer garden but the bar area is cool. I ask for a gin and tonic. The barman asks me for ID.

I am forty-five, and after three days on the road, I look every minute of my age. He isn't serious, of course, so I ask again for a gin and tonic. He asks again for my ID. I stare at him. 'What's the matter?' he says.

I laugh and say that it's just been so long since anyone has asked me that question that I don't know how to react.

'Don't mind me,' he says. 'I'm just in a funny mood tonight.'

Then he asks me what kind of gin I would like, because they have several shelves to choose from. He tells me to come in, to step behind the bar and see. Cornered, he insists that I shake his hand. He introduces himself, asks for my name and wants to know if I'm staying upstairs.

He is trying to be amusing, but the joke is clearly at my expense. How was I supposed to take it? Was I supposed to simper? To believe that he meant it, and expose myself to ridicule? Flirt, and play the coquette? Instead, I ignore it. I request the first gin my eyes alight on and retreat to the other side of the bar. I take the proffered glass and tonic bottle, sit as far away as I can, sip my drink and pretend to busy myself with my notes.

I drink slowly to prevent looking rude, but I just want to get out of here. The barman's endless sour-edged banter and loud exclamations are clearly designed to get customers to look up, pay attention and interact. He makes several quips in my direction and seems to find excuses to visit areas near me, even though there are no tables to clear or other customers to talk to. Perhaps it's just his way of saying: look love, I'm a joker, no offence! But I'm irritated that I can't tell him why his comments are inappropriate, why he makes me feel mocked and uneasy, why I feel obliged to sit and swallow the situation with my drink, which I cannot taste. Am I just a bad sport? Do I take myself too seriously? I don't think so, or at least I didn't, until I was lost for words.

When I lope off upstairs, the barman calls out for me to stop.

'What, are you leaving me?' he says. His grin is narrow, bitter.

He insists on shaking my hand, introduces himself for the second time, wants my name in response. I tell him, havering on the bottom stair, because he could easily make a fuss if I don't, and besides, my details must be in a room booking somewhere. I retreat, ensure that I don't need to leave my room again until the morning, and lock my door. I give myself a shake. I'm probably overreacting. But I've no idea who else has a room upstairs.

What irks me, what will return to me as I walk the next day, is that none of it would have happened like that if I was a man.

In the night the wind picks up, whipping the plastic ENGLAND bunting outside the window until it sounds like hail.

❖

Something has shifted on this part of the road. Where was it? When did it start? Maybe when the road became a conduit for industrial parks. Along the leafy lanes of East Kent, passing pedestrians smile. In the tourist centres of Medway, there are plenty of eccentric sightseers with backpacks. But this is straying into different territory, a pedestrian no-man's land. Or at least, no-woman's.

Along London Road I begin to notice truck-drivers staring at me. A man in a white van peers under his sunshade to get a closer look. Another clocks me through his open window as I pass. I am a moving scarecrow in Gore-Tex: why are they looking? Just because they can? At a crossroads outside Greenhithe, a flatbed trailer waits at the traffic lights, driver's window down and engine ticking. Behind the wheel is a man in his late thirties, singlet and sunburn, short blond hair and stubble-beard. In front of me a young woman is walking along the pavement in a T-shirt and shorts, long iron-groomed-and-highlighted hair swinging, a pink handbag in the crook of her arm. As I overtake her, I realise that the man in the trailer cab is looking at me and grinning. It is not a pleasant grin.

This is not flattery. I am not a more attractive sight than the woman I pass. I feel cold: a sickening, spreading gnaw. It takes me a moment to understand. The young, presentable woman is probably off-limits: spoken for, owned. But I am walking alone; clearly alone. I cannot be anyone's property, because if I was, I wouldn't be here like this. I would be wearing clothes that are for display rather than comfort, and carrying a handbag instead of a rucksack. One of us has somewhere to go, someone to meet; the other is unprotected on a long journey. Looking at me and assessing my chest is not going to offend anyone, is it? And if so inclined, I would be easy pickings.

After this I will really begin to notice it: the tit-staring. Further on, in Dartford, I'll pause to take in the art deco facade of the old cinema. Two passing men will pause to take in my chest. Afterwards I will check my reflection in shop windows as I walk: baggy grey walking trousers, long-sleeved base layer, peaked cap. Not a glimpse of skin. Not an ounce of provocation. But I am unescorted, a woman, and really, that's all that counts.

It's a little cooler first thing this morning, the air misted with precipitation. The front gardens of the identical semi-detached houses beyond Greenhithe are neat and proudly tended, geraniums in pots between the England flags. Sculpted shingle walkways surround pedestalled birdbaths. The gates are painted and trim. These sensible neighbourhoods feel sturdy and dependable, avuncular. The back gardens ought to contain greenhouses full of tomato plants, vegetable plots and rose bushes and attempts at topiary; home brew bubbling in the shed; the radio on low; conversations at Sunday lunch tables showing due diligence to family concerns, small movements of advancement, school cricket scores.

Maybe I am starting to miss people. Maybe I am projecting these cosy domestic arrangements onto the exteriors of houses because I am testing my independence and secretly, there is a still, small part of me that wants someone like my father, with woolly arms and an old jumper smelling slightly of bonfires, to make me a cup of tea. Maybe I just want such people to exist because in the last twenty-four hours, men have begun to morph into potentially hostile others. I am not used to such men; I am lucky enough to exist in a world of relative equality at work and at home, where being patronised or objectified is infrequent and, when it happens, treated as contemptible.

This morning will be made up of micro-shifts in my being, my sense of self moving like a wavering needle. I will fluctuate between feeling like a grown woman with self-determining freedom and wincing with pubescent, cheek-burning shame. With each unsolicited glance I will shrink a little, feel the edges of myself curl up and retreat inwards, attempt invisibility. At times I will feel vulnerable, as I did walking in my twenties, shrouded in a force-field of self-awareness, picking up on every external hum and quiver. It will horrify me, this regression; the reminder of a condition that we can so quickly and simply be reduced back into. But then I will grow outwards again, my curiosity a constant spur, the interest of the way bringing me back to my usual self. By the end of the day, this feeling will be just another facet of the journey, overtaken by something much more uncommon. Luckily for me, I am only passing through.

Aside from unwanted assessment, this part of the walk is full of unexpected pleasures and synchronicities. On this stretch, two semi-inflated, pink balloons are stuck in hedges several miles apart. Have they come from the same party, adventuring in opposite directions? In a neat mirroring, two hidden architectural prizes are the chief highlights at either end of the journey. One I am aware of, thanks to Merrill's guide; the other is a genuine surprise. Neither of them are directly on the route, but both will be worth a small detour.

❖

Commuters stride along the rat-run to Greenhithe train station. Many of them are pouring out of a dense residential area. Several of the houses and stacked flats in these mazy avenues and cul-de-sacs have sharp front gables with decorative corners, like little hip-high panniers, kicking out above the long skirts of front walls. There are sharp-pitched roofs. There are slim bay windows. Once I get to the heart of Ingress Park Avenue, I can see the source of these architectural cues. Above stepped banks of lawns that pour like a waterfall, white against the skyline, is Ingress Abbey. It's an iced confection of turret and castellation, a neo-gothic tower for a porch, projecting bays and waffle-textured chimneys. The roof is steep and slated. Box topiary flanks the entrance.

It's dolls-house-beautiful, this grand folly in the middle of a housing estate. The site is ancient – another lost priory, dissolved by Henry VIII – but the building is not. According to Historic England, this 'abbey' was created in 1833 by the architect Charles Moreing. It was built for a wealthy lawyer, James Harmer, who clearly felt deserving of a country estate. An alderman and something of a radical, Harmer was still traditional enough to want all the trimmings of a grand park, including grottoes, caves and a bridge.

The abbey was also home to another radical figure, the poet and Chartist reformer Eliza Cook. Cook was a proponent of social improvement through education and a woman who addressed much of her writing to the working class. Looking at the surroundings in which she wrote some of her work, it's easy to be sniffy about how comfortable she was while doing so. Gads Hill Place looks rather modest in comparison.

Still, I remind myself, sitting on a bench beneath this elevated pile, Cook and Harmer and Dickens and all of the other successful and comfortable Victorians with roofs over their heads and time to write could have been committed to the status quo. They didn't need to shout about injustices or strive for better working conditions. They didn't need to shame the complacent. They could have just sat in a wing-backed chair by the hearth and grown double chins. But they were self-educated. They didn't spend their childhoods up chimneys, but they were not manor-born. What would I have done if this was my home? Would I have felt the restless fire of inequality, or would I have taken up growing succulents in the summerhouse?

I take a photo of the abbey front and send it home. Right now, my husband and son are starting to bestir themselves for another school-and-work day. I am sitting in front of a manor house, feeling more than a little covetous, instead of hitting the London Road. I stand, stretch, shake myself. Today, I will reach the city.

And London does feel closer now. The route continues along the A226, breaking across the ring of the M25. There's a brief drizzle of warm rain, slight enough to evaporate within minutes, unworthy of waterproofing. Dartford, a bead on the rosary of pilgrims' stopping places, is the next major target. Chaucer doesn't mention Dartford by name, but then his pilgrims' journey is miraculously elided for the purposes of fiction. It's hard to believe that most travellers heading to the shrine of St Thomas didn't stop here at the end of their first day's ride. Full of religious centres, a bustling market town, it's an obvious place to break a journey.

❖

Away from the notorious Essex crossing, Dartford is surprisingly attractive. It is full of heritage hotspots for me to linger beside, nuggets of history to chew over. Here's the pub where the Kent hero Wat Tyler and his fellow rebels drank, before continuing to London to demand their freedom from Richard II. The River Darent, once a power source for water mills, feeds into the Thames from here, merging in a stretch of estuary. The 'ford' of Dartford provided an essential crossing for pilgrims on this way. Richard Duke of York surrendered to Henry VI here. Anne of Cleves lived in Dartford for a while, after her lucky escape from Henry VIII. The steam engineer Richard Trevithick worked and died here, carried to rest, so the cemetery plaque states, in a pauper's grave in St Edmund's Park. And here, just off the High Street, a blue plaque and heritage boards commemorate the 1908 Battle for Bull Centre, an unlikely stand-off between the police and the Salvation Army. Local Salvationists were jailed for their determination to preach the gospel nearby, in the teeth of public highway laws. According to the plaque, *the campaign for their release changed policing of public gatherings for ever.* I spot another plaque on the wall which, with no sense of irony, is dedicated to a local police constable in recognition of his services to the town.

Dartford also offers a much-needed toilet stop, where I find my relic of the day: a single penny piece, the bronze edges nibbled by use. *Spend a penny find a penny.* I pick it up in hope of luck.

My period has started, a week earlier than expected, and access to toilets will become the morning's obsession. I wonder, later, if this is indirectly related to the unwanted male gaze. Is some primordial signalling at work, some biological flag waving?

Two windows are painted onto the curved corner of a building on West Hill, showing some genuine trompe l'oeil skill. Aptly, it's the business premises of a picture framer. I carry the image of those windows with me on the long path out of town, willing them to reflect some real cloud cover in that flat, blue sky.

The sun is back, the temperature climbing. Beyond Dartford another long slog of roadside walking begins, but there are small distractions to be had. There is the quiet satisfaction of taking in another stretch of Watling Street, connecting back to Canterbury. This leg of the journey is certainly a psychogeographical dérive, Debord's 'rapid transit through varied ambiences'. Walking through Bexleyheath involves negotiating the shopping centre with its high-sided cinema complex. It's a mass of brick and steel dropped into the middle of the route: Watling Street is extinguished, so it's around it or through it. At least the shopfronts offer some shade, but this is soulless territory to be sped through.

On the other side, beyond the pound stores and supermarkets, the way returns to a sleeve of residential buildings lining the road. Busy bus routes and plane trees. Patches of parkland join the gaps. Leisure centres. Bowling. Football grounds. Welling and Crook Log and Shooter's Hill. The wedge-shaped Shoulder of Mutton Green.

The heat is fierce again. I stop for a pint of tonic water in the We-Anchor-In-Hope, where the business lunches are in full fried-scampi swing. I stare at my map: I'm almost touching the edge of Greenwich now.

❖

The road begins here to feel incongruously rural: the garden centre, the equestrian academy, the pocket community farm with its tangle of vegetable plots and small livestock, distant points of colour amongst the scarecrows and knee-high poly tunnels. I feel at home, but then this area is really just a limb of Kent, slowly swallowed by the cobra of the city. The etymology of Shooter's Hill is tricky to pin down. This place may get its name from the gun-work of highwaymen, taking advantage of Watling Street travellers and merchants. I prefer to think of it as the leafy practice range of archers, testing their longbows, playing at Robin Hood among the trees.

I feel oddly buoyant, lighter than blisters and backpack

and heat should allow. Perhaps this is a light-headedness, the point before exhaustion. Or perhaps it is some kind of self-defence: rising above the irritations of the morning, the discomforts of the body, an extreme opening up. Walking is an expansive act again, as on that first stretch leaving Canterbury. A liberation. Is it because I am alone again, away from the business of streets and sites, with just path and horizon and perpetual hedgerows? Or is this the promised pilgrimage stage of absorption into the landscape? Sensory observation has become acute. Details are crisp, as if haloed. That dandelion head is the yellowest of yellows, every petal limbed like the strokes in a miniaturist painting. I suddenly realise that this moment, and this, and this, is not something I envisaged doing, not a figment of my hyperactive writer's imagination: I actually *am* doing it. My dull body, my hungry senses, my mind with its focus and flits of perspective: all are wrapped up in this activity together; dogged, determined.

I'm distracted by towers on the A207. At the crest of Shooter's Hill, there's a glorious Edwardian water tower, just on the corner of Cleanthus Road, all red brick and cornices and octagonal extravagance. Then I'm set off course by a brown heritage road sign pointing to Severndroog Castle. I follow a path past a school playground and parking area, into the remaining pocket of an ancient woodland, Oxleas Wood.

Built in the 1780s, Severndroog is another folly, a memorial to Commodore Sir William James of the East India Company. Curious about the name, I later find out that James defeated a pirate fleet at the island stronghold of Suvarnadurg, in the Arabian Sea. Following his death, his widow commissioned the tower and named it – in a mumbling Anglicisation – after the site of his conquest. It's a neat little tower with hexagonal turrets and white-iced window arches; a grand, vertically-stretched gingerbread house. The wooden doors are painted liquorice black. The view from those upper windows must reveal a spread of city beyond the trees, but the castle is closed to visitors today.

I prowl the perimeter and peer up, in. I could rest here a while, take one of the plastic bucket seats from the café into the shade, listen out for squirrels in those ancient oaks, drink a pot of tea. But the café is closed too. I take a long draught from my water bottle. I could find another pub, perhaps.

No: this was a pleasant aside, a minor drift, but when I stop, I want to feel I've earned it. I'm edging closer to the city now, pressing at the perimeter, tipping over a ledge and down towards it. I retrace my steps to the road. I'm on the wrong side to enjoy the shade of a hedgerow, and as I walk on, there's a baked, shorn expanse of grass separating me from the edge of the wood. But reassuring road signs show Blackheath straight ahead. I let the slow descent roll me onwards.

❖

Beyond the crossroads there's a subtle shift: the railings seem blacker; the pavements broader; the trees taller, standing to attention. This is the Royal Borough of Greenwich, and the great expanse of the Royal Herbert Pavilion serves as a measure of affluence. Built as a hospital for Crimean veterans, the pavilion is now a seven-acre spread of luxury flats on a private estate. Rehabilitation can be bought here, in the heated swimming pool, spa and leisure centre.

At the end of the road, cars inch into the approach for the Blackwall Tunnel. I'm ticking off place names from a mental checklist now: Vanburgh Park; Maze Hill. The sun-bleached straw of Blackheath Common looks like a field after harvest. Carrion crows pick across it in search of worms and leavings. A shawl of pastel-soft bindweed is the only patch of colour, flourishing on a raised rough mound of overgrown spoil. The fizz of crickets is louder than the line of traffic crawling past.

The heat is almost solid here. One crow has found an empty can of Fosters and taps at the silver mouth in search of moisture. I pause beside it and offer assistance. The crow eyes me. I spot a drain cover a few steps away, with lozenge-shaped channels, where I pour in the last of my water. *There you go. Thy need is greater.* The crow looks unimpressed and hops away a few yards while I pass. When I look back it is standing by the drain cover, dipping and stretching that long black neck to drink.

Tonight's stop is on the Isle of Dogs, on the north bank of the Thames, so my route crosses over to the genteel, leafy walkways of Greenwich Park. The sudden shade carries the rich brewed-tea scent of bark chip. Jackdaws and pigeons are finishing a family picnic. French children delight in the sight of a grey squirrel at the base of rusty horse chestnut; it claws up the trunk out of reach. 'Maman, c'est la!' Litter pickers and park attendants drive about in their little crates on wheels. Just beyond the Observatory gates lies a small blanket of soft pigeon down, trailing larger pewter feathers like a boa. There's no carcass – the bird has escaped denuded or been carried off. The site of a fox catch, perhaps, or an errant dog that slipped the leash. Couples stroll past under avenues of lime trees.

It is glorious in the park. I could stay here, stretch out under one of those dappled limes, but I need to find my way to bed and board.

The final stretch of the walk means the beginning of Thameside tourist spots. The Cutty Sark clipper, black and gold, stretches across a smooth sea of paving, prow nosing like a mosquito's proboscis. The ship's belly slips beneath the glass wave of the visitors' centre, where afternoon tea can be enjoyed in a bloodless version of the colonial fashion.

It's a joy to be able to walk under the river. The Greenwich Foot Tunnel is an inconspicuous dome, a Victorian greenhouse on a red brick base. Inside, the murky glass takes on a fish tank feel. Descending the spiral staircase sends me through levels of increasing dampness. The air is tidal, the circular walls an acreage of glazed tiles lit by strip-lights. It could be a subterranean hospital corridor; a secret war tunnel; a portal to another, subaqueous dimension. Towards the far end the circumference narrows, the tiles replaced by rusty metal cladding. It looks bridge-like, all giant Meccano girders, bolts and seeping edges. A sign reveals that this is a reinforced, WWII bomb-damaged area.

A man walks through the tunnel talking to his young daughter. I can't help but listen in. It's her first time in the tunnel, but he knows it well. He tells her that he used this route every day to get to school. One misty morning, the river fog lapping at the stairwell, he went alone into the tunnel. There he saw a black dog standing in the middle of the space: no owner, no one else in sight. Then it was gone. 'You can imagine,' he says, 'how I wondered about that.'

A black shuck story for the Isle of Dogs. Yet he is still here to tell the tale.

It's an image to carry with me to The Ship.

❖

The pub's room offers luxuries that I have all but forgotten: a wide bed heaped with pillows, a sink, a fridge. I drink gin and tonic in the narrow courtyard garden and hug myself with glee. Later, there will be pizza hot from the wood-fired oven, football on in the bar, locals cheering for the French.

The first leg to Southwark is nearly done. I will look back at this day of walking with a sharpness and distinction that marks it out from all others. The freedom of movement and action, of transit through space, has become a distinct mode of being. There is the satisfaction of progress, the mounting adrenaline of approaching London, of nearing my first major goal.

Sitting in the pub courtyard, feet on the bench opposite, I cannot imagine myself before this began. My perception of time has shifted. Were there days, weeks, even years of my life when I was not walking like this? How could that be? The prospect of not doing this, of not rising early and walking a couple of hours before breakfast, feels alien. How will I cope when I'm back home, dealing with the demands of everyday? How will I function under the yoke of work, the short leash of the desk and computer? How will I bear being constantly in touch with, and at the beck of, other people? It seems impossible that such a thing could ever happen, or has ever happened. No obligation to speak to others offers a surging sense of independence, of self-containment. It counterbalances the unwanted stares, the raised heckles. It is a form of peace I didn't know existed. Have I, finally, merged with the landscape? Is my journey becoming an entity now? Or is this the lure of the hermitage, of the exile in the forest? If so, I might walk into the woods like the Pandavas, and stay for a dozen years.

I have gained something on the route these last two days; the miles feel genuine, tangible. I've made it to the city's edge, and it feels like an achievement. Pain has become banal: walking through the blisters until the feet are numb, it no longer hurts until I stop. Every pause is eased by rolling each foot in turn, like stirring a pot of paint with the toes.

After a bath I inspect the soles of my feet. The skin is toughening and there's an archipelago of blisters that, although burst, don't look too bad. Nothing that some strategically-placed blister plasters won't fix, I think. I leave my feet on top of the covers to air overnight, and once the football is over and the drinkers downstairs have dispersed, their voices meandering and diminishing into the surrounding streets, I close my eyes and sleep like the dead.

❖

No schoolchildren. No trade vans. Do people live here? Yes, because they were in the pub last night. On Westferry Road, a supermarket trolley lined with tinfoil serves as a tomato planter. Someone is watering those tomatoes, picking them, slicing them into salads. But the only people on the streets at this hour are the cyclists.

They appear in distinct swarms, aggressive and aerodynamic as wasps. They jump the red lights and cross no cycle zones, mounting pavements, wheels buzzing. Nearing the Greenwich Foot Tunnel, it's suddenly clear why: the lift is releasing them in batches, spitting them out through its grates, swallowing the next arrivals to disgorge them again across the river.

The tunnel suffers its own version of commuter rage: helmeted heads lowered, sunglasses flashing, the cyclists shove to be first in the lift, bikes held out like shields before them. In the tunnel itself they careen past, hissing, arcing, weaving across the central 'keep left' line. They zoom over the words 'no cycling' painted on the floor, the letters strobing in their shadows.

The phrase *foot* tunnel, *foot* tunnel plays like a mantra between my ears. There are too many cyclists to count. There are joggers too, aloof, lycra-armoured, ears and wrists and torsos connected by straps and wires. One wears a hydration suit that reminds me of Victorian corsetry.

This morning's walk is the final stretch of leg one. I'm wading into the city now, gathering myself for a first arrival in Southwark. The streets are restless, jostling, broiling; razor-wire and traffic and high-rise windows. This isn't a place for immersion in the landscape: there's just too much going on. I am firmly back in observing mode, but given that there's plenty to look at, I'm happy with that for now.

❖

Deptford Creek is a muddy disappointment of industrial wasteland and commuter traffic. No stepping-stone crossing place here; no ford to be picked across, staff in hand, testing the shallows. No rope ferry to straddle the last gasps of the Ravensbourne, tributary of the Thames, as it gives itself up to the river. The only other walkers here wear suits and earphones: not a single one of them is unplugged. There's a chivvying feel, a keep-moving-through, as if the ghost of Chaucer's Host is still calling over his shoulder at lagging stragglers. 'Lo Depeford, and it is half-wey pryme.' I'm so boxed in by buses and hoardings that I barely register when the street becomes a bridge. It could be dry beneath my feet, no hint of river beyond the channels of concrete and signage. Drake was knighted nearby. Ships were built here, then factories, and finally the power station. The Ravensbourne deserves its own walk, a pilgrimage to the source at Keston, but not today. A glance into the Creek's lost life can be spotted on a green oval plaque, inconspicuous against brick: the Greenwich and Deptford History Trail. THE DOMESDAY BOOK OF 1086 NOTED MANY WATERMILLS NEARBY. This morning, there are many transit vans.

Christopher Marlowe was killed not far from here, the eponymous *Dead Man in Deptford* of Anthony Burgess's extraordinary novel. A great reckoning in a little room, where Marlowe ate, drank, quarrelled and died. Marlowe's life started, like my walk, in Canterbury. Unlike him, it will continue beyond Deptford.

Marlowe stalks me as I walk. I sense him in my peripheral vision, wraith-like, accusing. In a house in Deptford Strand belonging to Eleanor Bull – not a tavern, as is often reported, but a private establishment – Marlowe took a dagger in the eye. The place may have served as a safe house for government agents like Marlowe and Robert Poley, one of the men with him when he died.

The murder was said to be an act of self-defence in a brawl over the bill, but the killer, Ingram Frizer, was a known liar wrapped up in shady dealings. It's highly likely that Marlowe was assassinated.

Marlowe's death also haunts the novel *Albert Angelo* by B. S. Johnson. It's a book I love and often teach; a brave, flawed, complex examination of inner and outer selves, steeped in the architecture and atmospheres of place. The eponymous supply teacher Albert, disgruntled and creatively frustrated, grapples with a world that, like many of Johnson's detractors – as with Marlowe – isn't ready for the risks he wants to take.

Johnson's book is not known so much for Albert's struggles as for being 'the one with the holes': in the third section of the book, a couple of pages are cut to frame a passage of upcoming text. These rectangular holes reveal part of a paragraph that appears later, but with the clever use of spacing, turning the cut pages does not give away the game. The reader's curiosity is piqued. What hovers, felt but unseen, behind these strange openings? Once we reach the reveal, we read these words:

> struggled to take back his knife, and inflicted on him a mortal wound above his right eye (the blade penetrating to a depth of two inches) from which he died instantly.

The text lingering beyond the holes is based on the Coroner's report into Marlowe's death. In Johnson's novel, this death loiters, waiting for the reader to catch up, peering back at us through the narrative that surrounds it. If we know the murder story behind those lines, then we have a complex relationship with time in the novel: what has been in the past of the world has yet to be in the world of the book, yet we still see it up ahead, have a precognition of it, like spying the tip of a distant monument. Is the monument Marlowe's genius? Or Albert's? Or Johnson's? Whatever it is, we don't understand it until it is lost. The text, like the holes, are a blip that the reader moves beyond when the revealed page is turned. The world carries on without Marlowe. There's just a gap where he used to be.

I carry Johnson's book in my head through the Deptford streets, turning over the connections. Albert is subject to intimidation by a group of boys who boast about how they 'got rid of' their previous teacher. He offers the class the chance to write down exactly what they feel about him without fear of recrimination, imagining that this will allow them to 'work out their hatred' without resorting to violence. Extracts of the pupils' writing, from the mildly abusive to the morbidly threatening, follow the passage about Marlowe's death. The blows Marlowe receives are nestled in amongst the threats of violence towards

Albert; the presence of the coroner's report foreshadows Albert's end. The students that Albert most fears will turn against him. It occurs to me that Albert is Johnson, and Albert is Marlowe: ergo, Johnson is Marlowe.

The real Christopher Marlowe lies in an unmarked grave in the grounds of St Nicholas churchyard. I keep looking out for the tower as I walk, and finally spot it reaching its squat neck into the sky. The church is just visible in a gap between the blocks of flats that line Creek Road: a glimpsed narrative, a dagger-thrust through the pages of the morning.

In a small staked area of grass, on an inconspicuous corner of Evelyn Street, are two dead foxes. They are juveniles, identical in size and colouring, set a slight distance from the low wall. They lie on their sides facing each other, eyes closed, tails raised. They could be dozing in the sun after a playful scrap, or locked in some game of dare, each waiting for the other to give in first and look.

A young woman approaches with a small boy in school shirt and shorts, a younger girl in a pushchair. The boy races ahead to look: he is checking on the foxes, making a study of them. He's seen them before; they have become a sign on the school route, like sweets in a shop window. He is excited, proprietorial, but also keenly concerned. The foxes look perfect, glossy, and far from decomposing. They must have died after the fierce weekend heat.

'Don't look,' says the woman to the boy. She shakes her head.

'It's such a shame, isn't it?' she says. 'I do wish someone would take them away.' The family think the foxes may have eaten something and choked, or been hit by the same car. They move on, the boy craning for a final peek, the girl safely shielded in her low-slung canvas chariot.

I think of these foxes, these vulpine lads, as I pass shopfronts and round corners. Siblings, sniffing out some supper, choking on splinters of the same bone or a shared, poisoned scrap. Racing each other to the far side of the road and bouncing against a single, speeding lump of metal. No marks on them, no signs of foam at the mouth. Staggering, crumpling, turning towards each other in disbelief. Lights out.

A moment later I realise that my cheeks are wet.

It's a shock to see so many small children walking and scootering alone, making the morning run to Deptford Park Primary School. It's quite the commute, just past the petrol station, along the A200 dense with traffic and litter, fag butts and fine grey dust and construction hoardings. On the far side of the road is a window with a neon yellow sign: BE KIND. Many of the school-goers smile shy hellos. Magpies chatter in a tree outside a small cluster of shops.

I picture the daily commute to my son's old infant school, past timber-framed buildings and a wall swagged with lilac wisteria, the sugared-almond smell of it in May sunshine, the narrow paths lined with window-boxes, the panes of glass above them bending and bottle-thick with age. It could be another country. Am I becoming maudlin today? Just affected, I think, deeply affected by everything. I could put it down to exhaustion, but I feel spry enough. Have I tapped into some secret, pilgrim's wellspring of compassion? Am I, finally, being moved by the journey in a mysterious way?

Perhaps. Perhaps this is another facet of the third stage of pilgrimage, this thinking about others and the tensions they bring. I am not travelling with anyone else, but I appear to have become an oozing sponge of empathy that sheds tears for dead foxes, Elizabethan playwrights, fictional characters and experimental writers. I'm welling up over children walking alone to school. I'm feeling sorry for this little boy that I'm about to pass, carrying a huge rucksack on his narrow shoulders and trying to balance when he stops at the kerb, lunchbox pendulous on a strap round his neck. I want to save him. I want to save everyone and everything, living and dead.

Dust and heat, dust and heat, and it's only just coming up to nine. At least there's Deptford Park, and further along,

Southwark Park. A pair of green lungs in this horseshoe bend of the river.

Between Rotherhithe and Bermondsey, the A200 becomes a simple feeder to Southwark Cathedral. But that would be too easy. I'm ripe for a diversion now, ready to drift and discover. I walk across a corner of King's Stairs Gardens to the ruins of Edward III's manor house. Once on the bank of the river, later with an added moat, these submerged stones sit at the foot of wide, shaved lawns. It's an odd collage of road, river and residences: a 'mews' of mean-windowed buildings, the flats of Cathay Street, a forgotten medieval palace. The outlines of the sunken walls have the feel of a hill fort, of fairy castles under the grass. The site has been filled in to prevent vandalism. What must it be like to live with this as your front garden? Do the patrons of The Angel raise a glass to Edward, the quarreller of Crécy, who ate and drank and flew falcons here? Do the locals picnic on this grass and see his son, the little Black Prince, playing tag round the ruins with their children?

Opposite are the bronze statues of Dr Salter's Daydream: a man with an umbrella, a woman with a spade, a girl and a cat. It's mysterious to me until I read the plaque: Alfred and Ada Salter's daughter, Joyce, died young, but they continued into old age, making good, nurturing the community, their Quaker faith and firebrand politics translated into actual deeds and tangible benefits.

I lean against the river wall and look down at the stony slate-and-purple muck of the shallows. Tower Bridge can be glimpsed from here. The path across the Thames stretches north-east, all the way to Walsingham.

❖

Bermondsey Wall Walk. Chambers Street; Flockton Street; George Row. Look straight up at the junction of these streets as you walk and you step into a Vorticist painting, all sharp cubist angles and dizzying skyward slants. Twisting, stepped and layered, the edges and ledges of architecture, the windows and roofs, suck you up and spin you round like a cyclone.

As I round the corner of Reeds Wharf I spot a man with trimmed white hair and beard, suit trousers and pressed, checked shirt. He pauses, bends over and picks something up from the floor. When he straightens, I realise it's a dog-end; he starts sucking at it to rekindle the smoke. It's only now that I notice he has bare feet.

Where has he emerged from? Is he an unlikely pilgrim too?

Perhaps he is a hapless office worker, sucked in by the power of the three waist-high standing stones over there, behind the cordoned bollards, amongst that scrubby patch of trees. Perhaps he went out for coffee and has awoken, like Thomas the Rhymer, into a world he no longer recognises.

Or perhaps he is an old resident of Jacob's Island, the Bermondsey slum. This is Dickens territory again: Bill Sykes was here, swinging from a rope above the foul Folly Ditch. The area is gentrified now, but it isn't hard to picture the local urchins, like Fagin's gang, scuttling along these streets with their bundles of swag, dodging the CCTV cameras.

Along Dockhead – how many times has that sign seen a can of spray paint? – a woman in a dark business suit looks up and grins. Her face is stunning, angular; her eyebrows, nose and chin a continuous line, arrow sharp. A face drawn by Paul Klee. A young woman cycles past: no helmet, but a red guard over her mouth like a hockey mask. Like a dog muzzle. A right turn, and this is Tooley Street, the final straight stretch to Southwark Cathedral. I take a deep breath – and then there it is, tucked beneath the flyover, modest as a parish church.

To get there, I navigate the overspill of London Bridge station: wheeled cases, elbows, dropped leaflets. I take my time now. I'm jostled and shoved, but find myself smiling. What is this? Patience? Blessedness? Smugness?

The heat increases the odours along this stretch: kerbside refuse collections, exhaust fumes, commuters in office shirts reeking of stale sweat and anti-perspirant. A few weeks ago, the route from Greenwich would have been alive with the scent of linden blossom. I've seen the green fruits swelling like filberts in the heat, the flowers now burnished dusty fragments in swept heaps by the kerbs. Aside from the smells of traffic and the faint savour of sea from the Thames, today's walk has been neutral. But here, nudging the edges of the cathedral, spilling out with tables, tents and teetering bar stools, is Borough Market: an explosion of frying onions, roasting meat, chilli, tomatoes stewing, mushrooms steaming, citrus, the lemongrass steam of spiced broth. It's a sudden but welcome assault. It's also a squeeze to get past the queues and find the visitor's entrance to the cathedral.

But I find it. Southwark Cathedral: the end of this stage of pilgrimage. How does it feel, arriving here? I could hug the steward who greets me on the door and offers me a souvenir guide.

Earlier, I spotted a discarded incense stick just along from a Chinese restaurant and considered it for relic of the day; it seemed fitting to carry incense on pilgrimage. But I left it there for passing dogs to sniff out and puzzle over. The cathedral guide is more fitting. I take it to the refectory café, ease my backpack into the chair beside me and drink two glasses of cold water in quick succession. Over coffee, I read the welcome to visitors from the Dean of Southwark, the Very Reverend Andrew Nunn. Southwark Cathedral, he writes, is one of those 'thin places where you can glimpse and touch a little bit of heaven'.

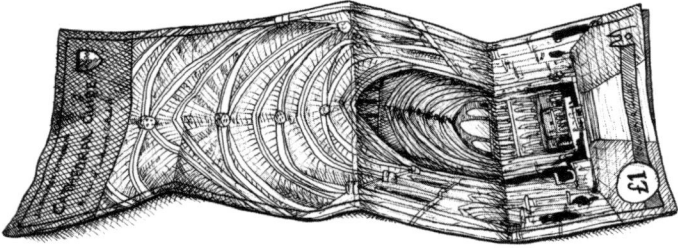

I have made it: I am officially in a thin place. I am ready to, as the Dean suggests, 'experience something of the hospitality of God'. I am also very ready to experience this piece of fruit cake.

❖

Inside the belly of the cathedral, a team of white-shirted men and women set out a series of round tables. There is the spreading of tablecloths, the clatter of cutlery polished and dropped into place. The cathedral will host a private dinner tonight, another taste of

God's hospitality, perhaps. The organ is tuning up, a reedy series of eerie notes bending and warping, coming together in a siren song. 'Gurdy strings!' a voice calls, and the pitch goes up another notch. 'Yep,' says the voice. The note changes. 'Yep. Yep.' Note by note up the scale, each key sounded by an unseen finger, pinched off by that disembodied 'yep'. It's the perfect soundtrack: gothic, wavering, uncanny.

The Harvard Chapel is surprisingly moving, a small silent space apart from the bustle of the nave. I light a candle by the 14th-century poet John Gower's tomb. The window nearby is dedicated to Gower's friend Chaucer. The stained glass depicts pilgrims on horseback, the monk in the foreground with enough puff to play bagpipes on the way. They are leaving Southwark for Canterbury, setting out to ride many of the roads I have just walked, but in reverse. This is their starting point, not an ending.

Doorkins Magnificat the cathedral cat is asleep on a cushion in the Chancellor of the Diocese's chair. The sign beside her advertises the illustrated tales of her adventures, a percentage of the profits keeping her in food and treats. Someone has left their chiselled traces on the stone pillar between the tombs of Master Pembroke and Bishop Edward Talbot. The dates and initials call out to be stroked by fingertips: H.M. S.T. 1911. Aged 17 yrs. A red round-faced devil – apparently a carved wooden roof boss –

gleefully munches the upper body of Judas Iscariot, the sinner's skirted tunic and legs protruding like an obscene, pleated tongue. I spend a while standing by the exposed archaeological chamber, risking a kind of historic vertigo: a chunk of Roman Road, the east wall of the 12th-century Chapter House, Norman Priory foundations. A 13th-century stone coffin is still in its original place, along with a 17th-century 'Delft' kiln, 18th-century York stone paving and 19th-century lead water pipe. There's even some sheet piling from 1999, presumably abandoned on site by a builder knocking off for the weekend. History, history, history, piled up architectural flotsam, the present peeled back like the lid on a tin of sardines.

The gift shop is layered and eclectic too, with its wire display racks and piped choral music. London tea towels, clotted cream fudge, lavender-scented toiletries and rosary beads. I buy some postcards to send home and a book about London's lost river Effra, weighing it in my hands before committing it to the rucksack.

I don't want to leave yet. I don't want to face the next leg of my journey. I'm afraid that walking across London, navigating the city crowds, will burst the bubble of my arrival. My feet don't hurt, my bloodstream is just the right level of caffeinated and I'm buzzing, basking in it, this delight in my surroundings. I don't feel cowed by the presence of the divine, but I do feel elated. I'm genuinely happy to be here, and I don't want to spoil it.

I have a final pee, another glass of water, and nip back to say farewell to Chaucer's window. His pilgrims are social as they travel the way, singing, storytelling, mocking and flirting. My walk has been very different. This lone, extended interval of psychogeography has made my rare moments of interaction – in a shop, on a footpath, in a café – feel rich and meaningful. I'm aware of an expansiveness and gratitude as I make my way down the nave and out into the sun. At this juncture in the journey I can recall many small, pleasant exchanges from the last few days that, at any other time, would be hurried and overlooked, forgotten. Lives bumping against each other in the swim of daily activity.

Is this a state of grace? Am I passing into the next stage of pilgrimage? Or is this a moment of secular sonder? In his online *Dictionary of Obscure Sorrows*, John Koenig defines sonder as:

> the realization that each random passerby is living a life as vivid and complex as your own— populated with their own ambitions, friends, routines, worries and inherited craziness—an epic story that continues invisibly around you like an anthill sprawling deep underground, with elaborate

passageways to thousands of other lives that you'll never know existed, in which you might appear only once, as an extra sipping coffee in the background, as a blur of traffic passing on the highway, as a lighted window at dusk.

Walking has brought renewed importance to my minor bumps and jostles with passers-by, the faces of strangers impressed, distinct, in my memory. For months to come I will be able to recall the features of people I meet on this walk: strangers that I speak a couple of words to, or who simply nod my way. It's as if the clay of experience is softened, moulded like dough by the repeated actions of moving and looking, of listening and seeking. Of walking, walking, walking.

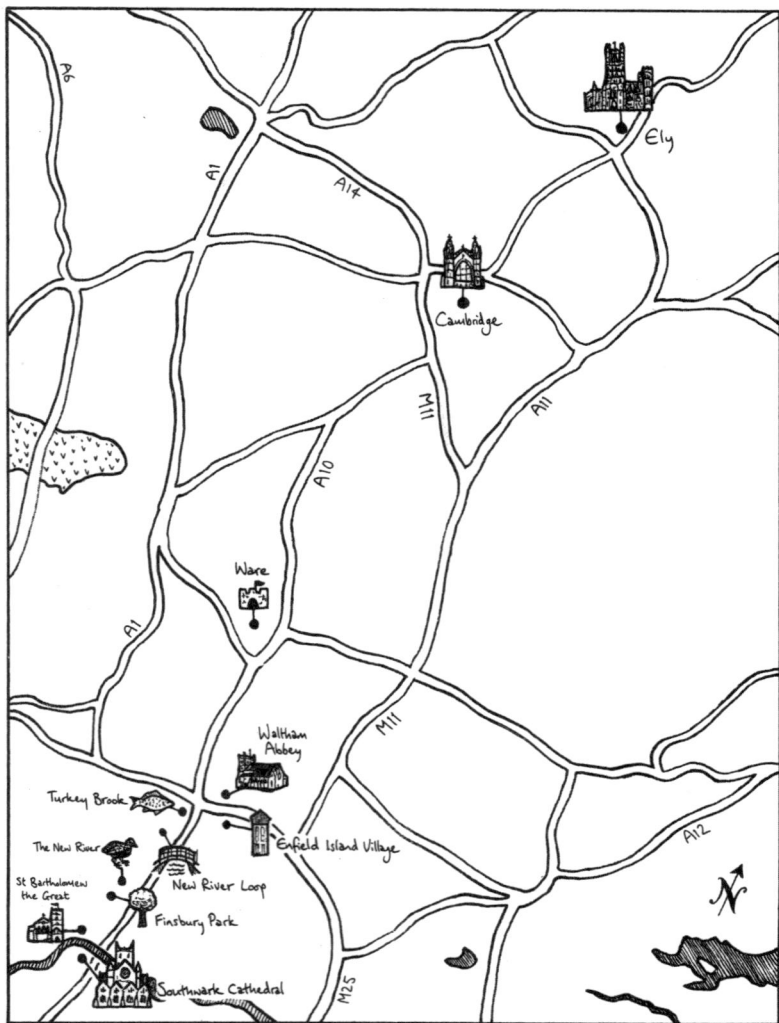

Map showing locations including Ely, Cambridge, Ware, Waltham Abbey, Turkey Brook, The New River, St Bartholomew the Great, New River Loop, Finsbury Park, Enfield Island Village, and Southwark Cathedral, with roads A6, A1, A14, A11, A10, M11, M25, and A12.

To Ely & Walsingham

WALKING INTO THE CITY IS walking into chaos. London Bridge. Cheapside. A tangle of weaving feet, bus fumes, cigarette smoke, irritation.

This is the beginning of pilgrimage leg two, cutting a long north-east line through Hertfordshire and Cambridgeshire to Ely. The rest of today will get me across London; beyond that, I've a long way to go.

The fire on the soles of my feet rekindles. I stop at a chemist for another hit of blister plasters and buy a couple of protein bars. It's only now that I realise how little I have been eating compared to a day at work or home. I'm burning the calories, but there are no regular meals.

I've not done this since early student days. It's hedonistic, but with a hint of the pilgrim's fast or the hermit's asceticism. There is unexpected freedom in this abstinence, of eating when hungry and not by the clock, or by times fixed by the appetites or schedules of others. Skipping meals is antisocial; eating together a form of ritual, a bonding, a needful element of family. Sharing a table at the end of a day or talking shop over a lunchtime sandwich are social contracts. Communal meals remind us of common ground and collective concerns. The problem is squeezing these moments into the routines of work and school, chores and sleep. We eat at our desks. We cram rather than savour. I must overeat all the time, the kind of publicly-enforced overeating that is negligible on a day-to-day basis. It's hard to imagine returning to that pattern of socially-induced self-harm, but I will do, soon, gradually reneging into bad habits, bending the body's needs to those of others, swallowing another little bit of self-will.

Food and flesh. I pass the Golden Boy of Pye Corner. I'm heading to Smithfield and St Bartholomew the Great, two sites of burnings: the reach of the Great Fire, the pyres of faith and obstinacy. The choice of saint feels apt, given that Bartholomew is often depicted holding his own skin, flayed and ready for the griddle. There's the smell of roasting, the sound of drilling, burnt afternoon odours drifting from the dark innards of the Butcher's Hook and Cleaver. The bar next door has steak and brisket on the menu, a smog of sacrificial grease in the air.

I want to admire the well-preserved Tudor Gatehouse of St Barts, but for all its architectural interest I find it sinister and oppressive, the portal to a dark past. This is slaughterhouse territory, a space steeped in the sounds and smells of despair: humiliation, grief, rage, roaring approval, roaring disapproval, bellowing animals. The buildings themselves have seen so much, the walls soaked in it all, witnesses to rebellions great and small, organised and individual. Catholics burning Protestants and Protestants burning Catholics; Lollards and Wycliffites; Recusants and Trinitarians. The deaths of writers, rebels and reformers. The indelible memory of martyrdoms.

A couple of names connect this spot and my journey from Kent. Thomas More signed off many execution orders before Henry VIII demanded his, putting that now-sainted head on a spike: the very head resting in a vault of St Dunstan's church in Canterbury. Wat Tyler lost his head right here, his Peasants' Revolt finally quashed after riding from the pub in Dartford that I passed.

A Scottish Saltire flag and bunches of flowers mark the site where the rebel William Wallace was hanged, drawn and quartered. Anne Askew, twenty-four years old, burned for heresy here: her offence was religious zeal and a rejection of male authority. Anne was carried to the stake on a chair, her joints still dislocated from the Tower rack, a torture session so profound that the Constable of the Tower refused to participate.

Hobbling. Breaking. Burning. Sacrifices based on divine faith or human justice. Punishments meted out by the same logic. Grumbling over sore feet seems laughable.

I'm taking the quiet back streets, keeping parallel with the A1. Through the narrow Cloth Fair, named after the notorious Bartholomew's Fair, swollen from its original purpose as a trade event. From here, the sideshows and stalls gained ground, spilling out into the surrounding parishes and growing increasingly spectacular until the fair became a byword for the sham and vulgar, a magnet for pickpockets and prostitutes. Given the violent entertainments of Smithfield, the lure of caged tigers, performing bears and freak shows come as no surprise. I pause for a hamstring stretch by The Charterhouse, taking in the stately crests and chimneys, arched windows and patchwork walls. Tourists dot the small, park-like centre of the square with its neat flowerbeds, its quiet sense of continuity. It's pacific here, away from the aura of Smithfield, the din of the fair long diminished. But these walls have seen plenty of turmoil too, shifting in use from priory to Tudor mansion to cloistered hospital and public school; dependent, like faith and gospel truth, upon the whims of State and rule.

I brace myself for a stretch of A1 along Goswell Road, but here, beyond the Barbican, the quiet is sudden, as if the rest of the city has just fallen off a shelf and taken with it all noise and busyness. A man passes by on the corner of Pear Tree Street, his distant cough an audible, echoing bark. There's a separateness to the stretch towards Islington, a sense of stasis. Small pockets of sound pop and dissolve between the bus stops and glassy reception foyers. A carpet of afternoon quiet, of mid-week out-of-window-staring; the countdown to August holidays; the prospect of a tea break. Islington is a caffeinated contrast: boutique hipsterdom, gym bodies. The white noise of baristas and moped deliveries. The fizz of harried commerce.

❖

A man begs for change on the pavement outside Highbury station, baseball cap shading his face, a paper Subway cup held up in one hand. At the bleep of a car horn he stands and tips loose change from cup to trouser pocket. Then he climbs, grinning, into the slick white leather passenger-seat of a waiting convertible.

Highbury Place starts with a green plaque, noting that Walter Sickert ran an art school and studio here. Highbury Fields, and the view from Sickert's windows, includes a pocket of woodland with a lone, magnificent foxglove. It's quiet again here, the trees still, the air hushed. Quiet, but slightly skewed. The world contains something of the queasy green-and-yellow glaze of a Sickert canvas this afternoon. Something rather Camden Town Murders.

My feet are not just burning now. Alongside the inevitable, damp-sock walking of high summer is an altogether more sinister squelching. Inspecting the source would involve too much logistical fuss: the unpeeling of socks, the public display of wounds, the application of fresh plasters. I trudge on, jaws clenched, heading north, my walk edging into a limp, my right leg lifting giddily away from the uneasy, shifting contract between gravity and ground.

There's an ice cream van parked in the middle of this long, park-side stretch. I speculate about whether numbing my tongue might quell my feet too – a kind of lolly-induced sympathetic magic. I order a cola-flavoured ice and suck it as I lope along. The cola has a strange edge to it, like disinfectant, but it's not enough to trick my feet.

The terraces are ornate here. Young women push prams and strollers built to tackle serious off-roading. At the corner of Highbury Grange there are lilies in full flower, soap-shop pungent, nodding their soporific heads against the green railings. The gates of the St Joan of Arc Primary School are, with no apparent trace of irony, liberally decorated with fire access warnings and smoking prohibitions.

It's the last mile of the day. I should be looking out for places to eat tonight, but already I know I won't make it back this way. Once these shoes come off they won't go back on. I would prefer not to eat than add extra mileage to today. There are chip shops and cafes, noodle bars and pubs, but the spectre of Sickert is hovering. Every shopfront and sign swims before me; every menu-laden window and porch awning is bottle-blent and smeary. It's like looking into a dirty fish tank. It's like drinking greasy tea.

I make it along the short stretch of Seven Sisters Road and into the hotel, trailing echoes of Smithfield in my wake. My room is cabin-small, the shower icy, and a group of men are simultaneously drilling and cooking barbecue outside my ground floor window. When I peel off those socks the plasters come away too. The sole of my right foot is butcher-shop raw, graphic as a penny dreadful.

Dinner will be a tub of hummus, earned by limping, Little Mermaid-like in plastic sandals, as far as the petrol station a few yards away. The night will come, and pass, and in the hours and days and weeks that follow I won't be able to recall a moment of it.

❖

The south side of Finsbury Park is hidden behind crash barriers. Dogs Patrolling warnings, portaloos and banks of rubbish. The sign above the Majestic Hotel is missing half of its letters.

Today brings riverside walking. Beyond the park is the New River Path, a long distance footpath following the artificial waterway, first constructed in the 17th century, to supply fresh water to London from the River Lea. Stoke Newington is a tempting nearby detour. I'd planned to stop there yesterday, but the prospect of an extra mile defeated me. I stare at the map again: Finsbury Park, Palmers Green – more pilgrimage lore? – Enfield Wash. Stoke Newington would add another couple of miles, tracing a triangle back to the top of the park before I can join the New River again.

I want to seek the inspiration for Arthur Machen's short story 'N'. Machen, the walking writer and a seeker of thin places, sites a fragment of paradise in the Stoke Newington suburbs. In 'N', three literary ramblers swap tales of the city over glasses of fireside punch. One of them retells the legend of Canon's Park, a forgotten space that maps no longer record. A tale-within-a-tale follows, building the legend of the park which, viewed by characters deemed insane or occultist, appears Edenic and otherworldly. Here are impossible flowers of silver and gold, a bubbling well and fantastic architecture. To others the site is just an unremarkable parterre surrounded by terraces, but old men of the town recall boyhood fears of the park, an eerie quality beneath a humble surface. As one of them says: there's quiet, and quiet. This otherworldly Canon's Park doesn't exist, but Clissold Park, Paradise House and Paradise Row were real enough. Did Machen gain a glimpse of heaven beside Green Lanes? Is Canon's Park really Clissold Park? If so, this could be the thinnest place of all, a threshold of the beyond. But even blanketed by early-morning paracetamol and double socks, I cannot face retracing my steps.

Finsbury Park is alive with acute sounds: rustlings in trees, gunshot cracks of twigs. Fellow walkers are distant figures. I feel the primal forest sense of watchers beyond the bushes. A man lurks behind a tree. Is he waiting for a dog? Or a deal? A green and yellow ring-necked parakeet swoops overhead. A jogger pauses to stretch by the outdoor gym. A tiny rabbit flattens its teacup body under a fence and wriggles into an invisible hole.

❖

The New River is a still canal slicked in lime moss. A large coot preens on the bank: beside the coot is a female mallard duck and a brood of hybrid chicks. In Alroy Road, a grey slab of building with ornate crest and curlicues is a neo-gothic secret lair and a car repair shop. This is a place of meetings and mergings: perhaps a little of Canon's Park aura has spread this far.

The New River plays hide-and-seek along the rungs of the Harringay Ladder, a neat series of parallel residential streets running between Wightman's Road and a section of Green Lanes. The river resurfaces with the lush vegetal smell of still water, a gated mouth lurking behind high green fences. On this stretch is a church, a mosque and – according to the sign in his window – a Master Psychic, operating from a basement in the shade of Jewson's building supplies.

A burst of birdsong replaces the rumble of the main road. The river is flanked by the backs of houses and the railway line, but it suddenly feels remote. The surface of the water is treacle-dark, the occasional white dab of coot forelock the only point of light. Further along it becomes clear and rippling, shallow enough to see the sandy riverbed from the strip of path. At a footbridge, tiny bubbles on the surface reveal the slate stripes of minnows and speckled fins of gudgeon. Darker shapes glide deeper, along the bottom.

New River Avenue is lined with smart flats: desirable views of the waterside from the upper storeys, coastal rattan furniture on the balconies. A man in white shorts leans against a second-floor railing, mug in hand, a holiday figure. The grass around the pump house is crisply shorn, the wide shingle path emitting a beach-like hiss.

There are no nightingales in Nightingale Gardens, just a sole magpie turning over last night's chip wrappers like a maid turning down beds. The air is tinged with the aroma of early-morning pot smoking. A bramble patch has sprouted up in a clump of weeds, the berries already glossy and fattening in the July sun. A dog walker is dragged along by seven cocker spaniels, a hydra-headed mass of flapping ears, tugging at the leash. The river has gone underground again, worming its secret way beneath tarmacked roads and grassy leisure spots.

Where the river is piped and invisible it is still tangible beneath turf and pavement, the swell of water like a magnet drawing the feet. I stop looking for the occasional footpath signs and trust to this subliminal dowsing. I take a short diversion to the shops of Palmers Green in search of breakfast and find a Greek bakery on a corner. It's a quiet space, a cornucopia of seeded breads and stuffed pastries, twisted dough and glazed buns, the smell of yeast warm in the air. The woman behind the counter handles each item with maternal pride, wrapping loaves in paper, a tucking-in. I buy a *flaouna*, a giant golden envelope of dough, cheese and raisins. It's dense and thick, heavy as a small brick in the top of my backpack, but irresistible. It will last me for days, this gilded slab: when I unpack I will find the final crust of it in a side pocket, hard as rind, wrapped in its paper shroud.

Towpath walking. A tiny dredging vessel slowly dub-dubs its way upstream, clearing weeds. A grey heron breaks its sentinel pose on the far bank, raising a pterosaur beak to eye my approach. It lifts a few inches from the ground and beats its way further up river, a repeated game of leapfrog that takes it a few yards ahead of me each time I gain ground. A black and white cat, a third of the size of the heron, crouches in the long grass to watch our strange dance. Eventually the heron gives up, soaring away with a yell, gliding over a back fence to terrorise some garden wildlife.

The river comes to life, reflecting patches of sunlight and overhanging branches, inviting enough to paddle in. There are gangs of mallards with extended nurseries of ducklings; Canada geese in cruising pairs; skittering moorhens. A hamlet of coot nests, woven from strips of cardboard and hedge trimmings, is populated with scrabbling youngsters testing out their webbed propulsion. The clipped clarion calls of the adult birds echo against the wall of trees. The water's surface is pocked with pond skaters; dragonflies and damselflies hover above. On a fist of ivy a mayfly warms its gauze wings, scorpion tail writhing. The insect life of the river is a bestiary of miniature mythical creatures, of wriggling manticores and buzzing, long-bodied wyverns.

It's an aspic moment: this part of the river walk, this day, this sunlight. Some experiences do that, enduring with a startling clarity, their shapes and colours oddly preserved in the gel of memory. I know this is such a moment as it happens, drinking it in, and it does stay with me, vivid and tangible and with just a hint of pain-negating rose-tint. It is a salve on the sore of the previous night, erasing the off-kilter weirdness of Seven Sisters Road. There may also be something hallucinogenic at work, a toxin in the blood. For now, I'll take it, whatever the cause.

❖

The knot of Enfield Loop is where the river traffic meets: chattering ducks, watchful herons. Graylag geese and mute swans. Smaller waterfowl glide across the pea-soup algae surface, Sunday strollers in a green park. A young family have come to watch the ducks; a retired couple have set up deck chairs in a patch of shade and are pouring tea from a thermos.

There are numerous down feathers scattered along the path, evidence of the everyday bustle. I pick one up as a relic of the day; cotton-candy soft, flecked with cream and brown. I put it in my back pocket for safekeeping, but it will be gone over the course of the day, lost on the route or whisked away by a draught into an unseen corner of tonight's hotel room.

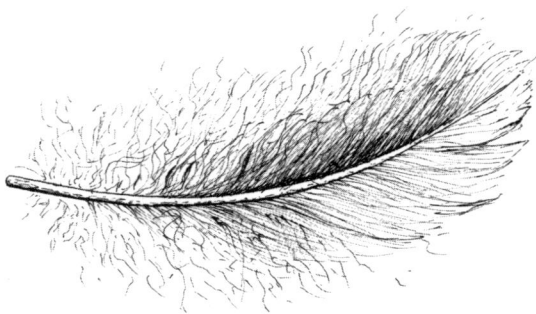

Gaining the next stretch of river means walking through residential avenues, the sounds of a sports day in the playing fields beyond breaking through spaces between houses. Amplified by the buildings, the cheers, chants and firing of the starting gun sound like distant battle.

I cross the main road to rejoin the river path and notice a young man in a black-hooded tracksuit up ahead. He swings a plastic Tesco carrier bag as he walks, pauses by the kissing gate to the river path, looks up and down the road, and goes in. There's something decidedly shifty about his body language. I pause for a moment. Should I reroute? I don't want a confrontation. This man clearly doesn't want to be followed, or at least, he's doing something he doesn't want anyone to see. But I shouldn't judge. Besides, this is my path. I'm not going to miss out on the river walk.

I cross the road and start along the towpath, holding back to keep the man ahead of me and in my sights. Black headed gulls wheel above the river and disappear beyond the far footbridge. The man suddenly stops. His stance is hunched, his back to me, but he seems taut. Ready to spring. I glance around and notice that we have reached a gap in the houses. This spot is not overlooked. The road is a good way behind; the bridge is a fair sprint up ahead. The man spins round to face me and drops his plastic bag. The bag lands on a raised drain cover, shrunken, depleted. He's holding something, something like a small rock. He clenches it in his left hand, hanging by his knee.

My neck prickles and I freeze for a moment, rapidly calculating a retreat. I can feel the blood in my wrists, the adrenaline kicking in. But as we stand there, staring across the distance at each other, something shifts. There's a softness to the scowl beneath that hood, something meek about the face, framed by the oversized cans of those headphones. That stance looks more defensive than aggressive. Maybe I've interrupted an exchange, and I'm not the customer he was expecting. I decide to walk on, to pass him, sizing up the distance to the footbridge. I could run that far if I have to – it's closer than going back to the road. If I get to the bridge I can be seen, attract attention if I need it. I take a slow breath in and out, and walk towards him.

The man watches me approach. I look down as I pass, giving him as wide a berth as the river bank and path and verge allow, clocking his distance in the tail of my eye.

I keep my eyes on the path. I keep going. Nothing happens.

A few yards along I turn back to check if he is following. It's now that I see what is in his hand. It's a heel of bread. That scowl was not a threat, but a defence: I've embarrassed him in the act. He has stolen down here to feed the ducks.

❖

The river path kicks away for a stretch. I pass Enfield Crematorium, manicured and maintained, serene against the wash of the A10. A large area of the site is like a well-tended park, a good spot for a picnic. For a site of collective losses and griefs, it's surprisingly pleasant: small dedicated shrubs and memorial benches, a monkey puzzle tree with a modest commemorative plaque. The formal headstones feel almost showy in their regimented rows, all polished granite and white chiselling. Some have ceramic photo plates attached to the black uprights, the faces of the buried smiling out in full technicolour. Inscriptions have become euphemistic: 'sunrise' and 'sunset' next to the birth and death dates, as if the loaded words 'born' and 'died' are too distasteful for public view. The vertical metal spikes of fencing flicker as I walk, the stark sunlight strobing. The graves and memorials bob up and down like the scene on a zoetrope. The early afternoon heat shimmers. I need to stop, to drink some water and break a little further into that lump of flaouna.

Beyond the cemetery is a small grassy slope, a tree, some simple benches. It turns out to be another memorial site, though a makeshift one. A cluster of desiccated flower bouquets – some still bearing their shop stickers and barcodes – are poked between the railings around the tree. Empty beer bottles lay scattered at the base, the leavings of libations or a farewell party. I sit on a bench, shrug off the backpack, arch my back. I eat a little, but only enough to line my stomach for more painkillers. I've managed roughly ten miles since Finsbury Park, much of which was softened when the morning's paracetamol kicked in. The towpath made for stretches of shock-absorbed stepping, facilitating my moment of serenity. My limbs and back are bearing up, but now that right foot is throbbing. There's only three or so miles to go, depending on where the hotel really is. I heave myself up, look again at the map, and promise myself an early evening glass of wine.

Past Turkey Street Station, my route follows Turkey Brook. I'd hoped for a connection to the country or the bird, but the etymology of the area proves disappointing; most likely the corruption of a local name such as Tuckey. The brook itself is a dank, scum-filmed brown channel rimed with plastic flotsam. Footballs and tennis balls are rotting buoys choked by weed, lost from the neighbouring gardens and recreation ground. Despite the rubbish, the channel is home to a family of moorhens and one giant goldfish, swollen to become the mottled ruler of this murky backwater.

Away from the houses the water begins to clear again. There are more mallards, Aylesbury ducks, damselflies, yellow waterlilies in full buttercup flower, the obscene pokers of bulrushes. Great banks of lilac and pink flowers are a welcome splash of colour, but these sugary, orchid-headed invaders are Himalayan balsam, an exotic escapee. Despite this, I can't resist pausing to admire them, soaking up a little of their sweetness, resting my eyes. A red kite hangs in the air above the railway crossing, watching for movement in the long grass. A corvid feather, a peacock blue and green shimmer above its charcoal base, lies in the centre of the path. It catches the light like oil in a puddle, like burnished enamel. It's so miraculous I decide it deserves to be carried like a relic too.

❖

Enfield Lock feels like the furthest reach of Greater London, the edge of the plate, the lip of the M25, beyond which the rest of the country begins. The path connects with National Cycle Route 1 and there are long recreational trails from here on the London Loop and Lea Valley Walk. The flat strip of canal and painted lock gates speak of narrowboat holidays. It's all out there, waiting to happen: North on the Lee into Hertfordshire, branching east into the River Stort. Escape, the romance of the waterways, the little moorings in arcs of light from cheering riverside pubs.

I sit on the steps by the lock and stretch my legs, roll the ankles to ease their aches. A narrowboat pulls up and a young woman, solo crewing, leaps out onto the path. She runs back and forth, winching and winding ropes, cursing and laughing. I would offer to help but I would be more of a hindrance, and there's a fierce joy in the woman's face as she works the mechanism, swearing at the rapid rise and fall of the lock water.

This is the last push before tonight's stop in a roadside, chain hotel. The thought of a clean, wide bed in an anonymous room is enough to get me moving again. I spot the white-iced Lee Conservancy, the old toll office, and beside it the neat terraces of Government Row. These houses were the homes of workers in the Royal Small Arms Factory, creators of muskets and sniper rifles. The nearby garden of Gunpowder Park was once the test firing range. It's all pretty and harmless enough now, but it's not long since this area stopped making and shipping out military assault weapons and experimental munitions.

Enfield Island Village, once part of the factory complex, has been recast as a housing estate. It is classic brownfield development; neat brick homes, riverside gardens, cul-de-sacs and marked parking bays. The River Lea runs through the island, and crossing it means stepping into a world of pocket woodlands, nature reserves and the lakes of disused gravel pits. This is good hedgerow country for foraging. I sample a couple of early blackberries, still sharp-juiced and hairy. I've reached the recreational walking path now, sending a signal for my foot to reach its final stage of revolution. Like yesterday's swansong along

Highbury Fields, my walk is reduced to a limp, rolling the ball of my foot to avoid the pressure.

It doesn't take much of this lopsided gait to damage my right ankle too: hot and swollen, it begins to buckle with the impact. I leave the shady scrubland and enter the full blaze of the final roadside stretch. The hotel is along this road somewhere, beside a pub: the sign of The Plough screams with possibility, but there's another interminable 300 yards up a slight slope before I see tonight's stop. The relief is enormous, but crossing the car park to check in is impossible without stopping at the pub first.

The darkness inside is so absolute that for a moment I could almost touch it: a soft wall of dust and the tall shadows of bar furniture. Fruit machines blink and plink. I order a pint of tonic and soda, drink half of it without coming up for air, and perch on a high bench to consider the menu. The thought of sitting down to a meal –especially something as vast and solid and potentially oil-slick as the bar meals listed here – is utterly alien and repellent. Still, I reason, by tonight I will feel differently, and I'll need food to soak up more paracetamol and that fat glass of promised wine. I finish my drink and pick my way across the giant dustbowl of car park. Surely no car park needs to be this vast.

I check in to the hotel, get up to my room and as I open the door, reel back from the smell of trapped cigarette smoke.

Changing rooms will mean going back to reception – the hall, the lift or stairs, then back again – and for a minute I hesitate. But the smell is too much, the window barely opens to release it and I'm starting to sway on my feet. I need to stop. I need to lay down. Getting back to reception feels like the traversing of mountains, but the receptionist instantly offers me another room and a change of key card. Once I'm back upstairs, along the corridor and into the neighbouring room it all feels worth it. I remove my shoes and, tentatively, socks. I shower in ferocious hot water, lay on the bed in a damp towel, air my ragged feet and stare at the ceiling.

I am floating. It's as if the aching of muscles and peeling away of tattered skin have led to a heightening, a levitation. I'd like to think this is a spiritual reward for scourging my body, a pilgrim's trophy. But by the swelling of my big toe, and the alarming seepage between blister plasters, I'm beginning to suspect an infection.

I consider visiting the pub in hotel slippers. It's the prospect of tarmac under the cardboard-thin soles, rather than a sense of decorum, that stops me. Whatever the state of me, I will eat a meal tonight. And I will have that glass of wine.

❖

I wake up to a sensation of heat. Despite a night's sleep, that right foot is raw and burning. The nail of the big toe is the dirty yellow of a used duster, slightly sunken in the swollen mass. The space between this toe and the next has disappeared. Territory has been gained overnight, the morass of blisters spreading across the ball of the foot like grease on water. The whole thing is damp, torn, angry.

The medieval pilgrim accepted pain as a necessary element of pilgrimage, a penitential scouring that brought them closer to God, moving Him to mercy. Suffering was a welcome sign of spiritual renewal. I have access to modern comforts and conveniences to help me cope. I take two paracetamol with a swig of hotel-room coffee. I cover the offending areas with my five remaining blister plasters, sealing down the edges with strips of fabric plaster to contain the mess. I inch on a second sock for extra padding. At the last moment I push the whole bundle of foot into a shoe and lever up, cursing.

Suffering and pilgrimage. Pain and penance. 'It cannot be doubted,' claims historian Emma J. Wells, 'that medieval devotion towards the cults of saints was a physical affair'. A belief in the reward of divine mediation must have been a constant spur on the road; risking the loss of that chance too great a price to pay for giving up. I have other things at stake. I won't get this opportunity again any time soon: to walk alone, to explore and think and write on the path. I'm not going to let the contents of one shoe prevent me. The medieval pilgrim would run far greater risks than me to achieve their destination: walking, riding, sailing, sleeping in lice-ridden beds, sleeping rough, sleeping in churches, passing through dangerous terrain, risking cutthroats and cutpurses and, once at the shrine itself, 'even crawling', in order to gain 'direct contact with the intercessory power of the divine.' Proximity to the shrine of the saint is imperative. To be near a sacred tomb or relic is to gain access to miraculous powers. To see it from afar is one thing – to touch it is consummation. I will get to Walsingham. I will enter that shrine. If a footsore medieval pilgrim can make it, why not me?

Between the secular outside world and the sacred heart of the shrine is the threshold space of the church, priory or chapel. Once inside the door, the medieval pilgrim would be expected to wait in line to access a popular shrine, a series of gates and screens shepherding the faithful towards the inner sanctum. To gain entry to the shrine was to pass through these boundary markers, like the Tensa barriers at airport customs or a Post Office in the run-up to Christmas. Passing each marker meant edging closer to God. Arriving meant making it through that thoroughly English liminal space, that national state of limbo: the queue.

I am in limbo. Today I will be doomed to wind my way, labyrinth-like, back and forth, to traverse a small space with a circuitous route. I will be a pilgrim following the path between those Tensa strips, uncertain of whether I am making progress or am just the butt of some elaborate practical joke.

I won't know this until later, of course, when I am washed ashore from the shipwreck of today. Then, I will think of the writer W. G. Sebald and his book *The Rings of Saturn: an English Pilgrimage*. Lost in the convolutions of Dunwich Heath, Sebald's narrator (Sebald himself? Sebald's alter ego?) walks, as I will today, as if in a fever. In a dream, he sees the labyrinthine confusion of heath and hedgerows from above, and it seems to be a cross-section of his very brain.

On the ground, in the moment, the path and its purpose can become obscured. There is a map, a way through, and somehow, an innate knowledge of this – but it can only be viewed at a distance.

I need to get moving. It's going to be another fierce day of heat, and preparing my foot has taken up valuable walking time in the cool of the morning. Every right step lands on a stovetop. I limp out of the hotel towards the main road. Today's route takes in Waltham Abbey itself. Beyond that is the walk to Ware. It's a stretch of roughly fifteen miles, mostly along the riverside.

Getting to town means crossing a busy link road and walking a stretch beside it. There is no path from here, only an uneven grass verge with patches of grasping brambles, hawthorn and nettle. Heavy trucks lumber past. I lope over to the cycle track on the opposite side, where the added width is a boon, cushioning the swoosh of passing lorries.

I turn left at the roundabout. But it doesn't feel right.

I don't feel right. It's probably just the pain.

When I get to the town I can get more plasters, maybe some foot powder. Drink some juice and rest a little before the towpath.

No. I'm heading the wrong way. Is that the town? A church tower?

No, it's a reflection. Glass then; offices, or a garden centre. Not this way.

I retrace my steps to the roundabout and look back. How far did I get along that road? A cyclist passes, gaining the spot where I paused and turned around within seconds. But I was walking for ages. Wasn't I?

Turning the corner is stepping off a carousel. Maybe I just need that juice. Blood sugar. Maybe I repacked my backpack badly, setting me at a slant. Maybe I need to eat something.

❖

It's a clumsy mile and a half before I reach the edge of Waltham Abbey town. There's a chemist in Sun Street, a distant point of salvation. I stock up, spending a small fortune on blister plasters, powder, antiseptic wipes and painkillers. I hobble to a café, order coffee and orange juice, take a long, bovine stare at the menu. My stomach tightens. No food. Maybe some foot powder will help. I retreat into the disabled toilet with the bag of chemist goods. The fabric plasters have already slipped and rubbed loose. Beneath them, the blister plasters are swollen lolling tongues that curl up and roll off, sated as leeches.

I sip my drinks alternately. A little juice: a little coffee. How seriously should I consider the horror inside my sock? Is this just what blisters do? Is this athlete's foot? I think of WWI soldiers in their trenches. I think of sheep in wet fields. I think of amputations.

I'm in the café for an hour, waiting for the painkillers to work, mustering my courage. Walking through the pain is essential. I've done it before. Those hot embers reduced once, didn't they? Yes, there are more of them now, but once I get going I'll forget all about it. I'm just a little light-headed. I leaver myself up and back onto the street: I'm losing precious time.

The abbey grounds are an extended park, another part of the landscape bearing Reformation scars. The Harold Stone, just outside the remaining church, marks the probable resting place of Harold Godwinson, the last Anglo-Saxon king of England. It's a fair trek from Battle in Sussex to Waltham Abbey, a long final journey. Is Harold buried here, in the church he fostered, or back at his birthplace in Bosham, Sussex?

I think he's here, lying someone near this slab. Harold took a special interest in Waltham Abbey. He was the Earl of East Anglia, with Waltham manor part of his estate, but he had also been cured by the holy cross of Waltham. The cross, long lost, once drew pilgrims with its renowned healing powers. Harold was one of its supplicants. In gratitude for its cure, he rebuilt the church here.

The sun is getting higher. I ask Harold if I should sit down for a bit. He directs me to a tree near some benches, a spot that's not too far away but affords some privacy. I obey and sit down in the shade. My foot is screaming, so I remove my shoe to let the air in and the scream out. My sock is wet, so I remove that too and lay it in the sun to dry. In fact, my foot is wet, but unfortunately I cannot remove that. Some more powder might help. I undo the work of the café stop, shedding plasters, disinfecting with wipes, dusting with powder. It feels like changing a nappy: didn't I just do this? Yes, and it's soiled already. And will be again. There are another dozen or so miles from here to tonight's stop, so it's worth taking precautions while I can.

King Henry was here too: Henry the second, Henry the Becket-killer. Part of his penance, as ordered by the pope, was to found new monasteries. Never literal in his promises, Henry re-founded Waltham as a priory, replacing Harold's canons with Augustinian priests. Perhaps he came here to see the work done. Perhaps he stood here, where Harold's Stone now stands, to see the tomb of the Saxon king. Perhaps he saw the holy cross of Waltham and its pilgrims and thought about Becket, once his worldly friend, now a Christian martyr. By then, the monks of Canterbury were already promoting the cult of St Thomas, setting up those barriers to manage the crowds, churning out pilgrims' souvenirs.

Time to explore. Waltham Abbey church proves to be worth every injurious step. A side door is open; within the great trunk of the nave a staff meeting is in progress. A dozen or so men and women in clerical and civilian dress discuss parking arrangements for an event. Several look up and smile.

The interior is a mix of medieval remains and Pre-Raphaelite flourishes. The celebrated ceiling is a gaming board of decorative diamonds, the slate-and-white gaps bright as fishmonger's tiles. Zodiac signs and labours of the months; a celebration of foliage and pattern. The Burne-Jones windows defy the usual treacle-richness of Victorian stained glass: this is spun-sugar, conservatory window glass, a wash of Mediterranean light, cerulean and bay-water green. There is the grooved South Aisle pillar, its stone scarred by chains where the church's holy books were hung for all to read: Erasmus on the Epistles, Cranmer's Bible. Foxe's Book of Martyrs. Pendulous arcs of time and use; reformation tree rings still there to be counted.

The Denny family tomb depicts a married couple, recumbent on left sides, propped in matching position for some reading before lights out, some gentle tomb-top spooning. And there is the treasure of the Doom Painting in the Lady Chapel: a gaping leviathan hell mouth, red devils bundling sinners like faggots for the fire, the blessed exalting with jazz hands at the gate of heaven.

The volunteer in the gift shop is delighted by my enthusiasm for this Last Judgement. She hands me more information about the painting, which was uncovered in the 19th century. 'It was hidden by a fake ceiling in the Reformation,' she says. 'They should have torn it down, but they covered it up instead, thank goodness.' A sober moment of political wait-and-see from the people of Waltham. After so many changes, why destroy something that had survived so long? The tide might turn again any moment. All it takes is a death. Or a marriage. And boarding it in is easier to undo than layers of whitewash.

I buy a postcard of the Doom Painting, a church guidebook and a pamphlet on the legend of that holy cross. The woman asks about my pack. I tell her of my pilgrimage and she enthuses about Ely and Walsingham. She is astonished that I am walking as much as I can of the route. I tell her that my blisters may get the better of me, but that I plan to walk through the pain today. That maybe the suffering is essential after all, par for the course. She nods sagely. 'God be with you,' she says. I thank her as I leave. I need whatever grace is out there if I'm going to get much further.

I stop at the public toilets opposite, gather my resolve and set out to find the River Lea Navigation. It's getting late – already after eleven – and heating up. In the last few days I've done the bulk of my walking by noon, dodging much of the afternoon sun. This is not a good start.

Keep going. Keep going. Keep walking, because the bite of those blisters will soften, as it always does. The painkillers will work. The muscles will relax. Keep walking.

I try to. I try variations to reduce the impact on that right sole. I walk on tiptoes, but it pulls at my calf. I walk on the outside of my foot, but it sends a dull ache up along my side, tugging at my groin and hip. I walk on the ball of my foot, but that hits me in the small of my back.

I make it across the road to the towpath. It is idyllic down here: narrow boats, swans, dipping trees with patches of emerald shade, a gravelled track to walk on…

A gravelled track. Miles of it: shark-toothed, shrapnel-sharp. An acreage of diamond points. A beach of razors.

I grit my teeth. I stumble on, hopscotching onto patches of grass whenever the path is wide enough. But it is rarely wide enough. I sway. The side-stepping and dodging is making things worse. Did I have breakfast? Did I have wine for breakfast?

Signs dotted along the way advise cyclists to slow down and 'share the space'. Like the Greenwich Foot Tunnel, this means nothing to those on wheels. Every few paces I am pushed aside as another cyclist speeds by. A small gap opens, long enough to gain momentum: I make it into the centre of the path just as it begins to narrow. But there is a clattering behind me, a tinny sounding of bells. A chattering of voices. I turn to see a flock of school children on bikes careening towards me, all in matching yellow shirts that must be bug-magnets on a day like this. I press myself into the trees to let them pass. Then there is another wave of children. Then a third.

Enough. What would you do, Harold? Harold would go into the trees, away from the hot arrowheads of towpath stones. Harold leads me aside to a short stretch of green trackway. It's a temporary respite: a few hundred yards of dappled light, a few moments away from sun and clicking wheels and bed-of-nails stepping. All too soon, the trees spit me back out onto the towpath.

Narrow boats along this route are in various states of decay, use and ornamentation. One shows the wreckage of the previous night's party, a pile of beer cans, unwashed plates and burnt-out barbeque tray littering the upper deck and spreading onto the towpath. One appears to be manned, but the faces in the cockpit are painted onto the heads of shop dummies; one dummy wears a captain's cap, tipped at a jaunty angle. Another boat is festooned with swags of washing, drying rigid in the midday bake. The most appealing boat is the one that's barely visible under the foliage of its potted roof garden. Runner beans, tomatoes, squashes, salads: a floating vegetable patch.

By one o'clock I've had enough sun. Counting down the canal boats helps to keep up momentum, but I urgently need more painkillers. I find a patch of shade, which leads to a picnic area, and fling down my backpack. It's a chance to air my feet, to see how far I've come. To consult the map. Except, I realise, with plunging dread, I'm not holding the map.

I haven't been holding the map for some time.

I remember holding my backpack straps with both hands

to steady myself. I wasn't holding the map then. Did I drop it? No. I would have noticed, because the map was in the map folder with my itinerary, and the brown paper bag from the abbey gift shop.

When did I last see it? In the public toilets. Of course. On the back of the door, hanging from that fraying black cord that I never wanted to put around my neck because it felt like being harnessed, but should have – stupid, stupid – because now it is gone. I left it, miles back, and I didn't notice. I have been so woozily distracted by my foot and so obsessed with not being distracted by my foot that I did. Not. Notice.

I break a rule of the trip and look at the map on my phone. I've walked about six miles. I should go back. Without the map I will miss vital elements of leg three, the Ely to Walsingham route. The itinerary includes all of the stops I need to make, the addresses and booking details. There is the bag of abbey guide books. I can go without the books. I can get another copy of the itinerary. But can I really continue the walk without that map?

I should go back.

I can't go back.

I can't walk back, retrace that path, do it all again. I can't.

I look up the abbey details, phone the visitor centre and explain. The woman who answers promises to search the church and takes my number to call me back. I send a message home and my husband emails me a copy of the itinerary. I try to eat some of the never-ending flaouna, but it's impossible to swallow.

I wait for the phone to ring.

It's getting late, and I've got many more miles to cover. I have to decide, to act.

I repackage the foot and heave myself up. If I keep going along the towpath I can take a diversion to the main road and pick up a bus back to town. I can regain my lost package and bus back again, get back to the path, carry on. It may lose me an hour of walking now, but it will save me trouble later.

Towpath, side road, main road, bus stop. A bus appears. Somehow, I have enough cash to buy a return ticket to Waltham Cross.

Riding the bus is like flying. Effortless gliding. The speed is intense, the lumps and crevices of the road blending into a soup of surface, the buildings beyond flickering into a seamless stream. It's an impossible luxury, this everyday event: the convenience, the forward propulsion. The condensing of time that can be spent staring, thinking; unmoving, yet moving.

From the bus station at Waltham Cross I pick up a shuttle to the edge of Waltham Abbey town. I limp back past the sites of the morning: this is the street I walked along. These are the offices

I passed. There is the abbey church. And here is the public toilet, the cubicle with the hook where the map bag will be hanging, mocking me – ridiculous me – for a moment's oversight.

It isn't there.

But it was. I know for certain now, recall every movement; hanging up that cord, washing my hands and looking for something to dry them on, stepping out of the door, shaking off the water. I was not holding anything then. I definitely left it here. And now it is gone.

Someone will have handed it in. It's no use to anyone else. I go back to the church; in the gift shop, the volunteer shift has changed and there's a different woman behind the counter now. No lost property has been handed in today, she is certain of it. I go to the Tourist Information Centre, where a guide takes my name and address and promises to keep me informed. I try the town hall. I limp back along Sun Street and ask in the Co-op, the Post Office, the museum, the library.

It has gone. Somebody has found it, rummaged through it, thrown it away.

I stare at the front of the church. I think of this morning's blessing from the volunteer there. God is not with me today. Today is a conspiracy.

It's mid-afternoon. I am back at the beginning of my

day's walk. My foot is a molten lump of pain to be dragged along beside me. I go back into the gift shop, buy a replacement set of guidebook, postcard and pamphlet, and walk away from town again. The street. The offices. The bus stop.

Enough. I have been ambushed by circumstance. I have tried to walk to Ware and I have been defeated. The prospect of the towpath rises up before me, a mountain of white gravel daggers. Hours of limping; eight or nine miles of it from where I stopped.

A bus approaches. I flag it down and show my ticket. But the ticket won't get me from here to Waltham Cross station. This route has a different service operator. The driver looks me over.

'Just sit down, love,' he says. 'I'll let you know when we're near the station.'

The bus moves, or perhaps the ground moves. There is movement, at least. Harold tells me that this is not the last I've seen of him.

A phone rings. The sound appears to come from somewhere inside me. It's my phone; my pocket. I try to remember what to do.

It's the woman from Waltham Abbey. 'Good news!' Somebody has found my map folder, and has handed it to the verger, who has just handed it in to the desk. Can I come back to collect it?

It was there all the time. It was in somebody's hand, somebody who was a few steps ahead of me, and then several minutes behind.

Back and forth. Back and forth. Waltham Abbey wants me to stop.

The bus driver calls out: we are near the train station. I'll get the package somehow, but not now. I apologise to the woman on the phone and assure her that I will come back for the map soon. Meanwhile, I have to regroup. I have to put out the fire in my shoe.

I get the train to Ware. It moves at such a shocking, blurring speed that it is probably a rocket. I get out and look for tonight's B&B; back and forth, back and forth along the same few yards of road. The door is, of course, there all the time, carried around in somebody's hand. The owner lets me in, makes me tea, laughs gently at my tale. One of the two house terriers climbs onto my lap. I could weep with relief. Now I can remove this shoe, shower, rest. Plan. Reset the day.

Tomorrow I can start again. I've missed out a few miles, but that's all. I've got this far. Maybe tomorrow I can make an early start, shuttle in and out of Waltham, pick up the map folder, get on the road. Get some more miles in before the heat begins.

Sitting on the bed, I examine the foot. It is red, blue

and black. It oozes. It smells terrible, even after showering and disinfecting and powdering.

The ball of my foot is rotting. There are sinister red lines running from the lowest blister to the middle of the sole, snaking around the ankle and moving upwards, into the calf. The venom is spreading. This is an infection, and it is planning to take over new ground.

I look up the local GP surgery and dial the number. They won't see me if I am not registered: 'no walk-ins', says the receptionist. No limp-ins. I dial the NHS hotline. I can hear my own voice echoing in the line, the quavering notes of hysteria just below the jocosity as I describe those red snakes. How silly they are, these annoying lines! How ridiculous I am to be creating them! I am told to hold the line for the clinical advisor. The clinical advisor tells me to get to the nearest Accident and Emergency department. To do it now. To be there within the hour.

'An untreated infection tracking like this can lead to complications,' she says. 'Serious complications.' The word 'sepsis' hovers unspoken between us. I explain that I am in a B&B, on my own, in a strange town, on a very long walk.

'I hope this doesn't put you off future walking holidays,' she says, 'but the only place you are going now is hospital.' I need to get a taxi, get a lift – get there somehow. A GP might be able to treat me, but I could need intravenous antibiotics. 'The sooner you get treatment, the better your recovery time.'

❖

Walking and observing, time becomes dense. There are so many layers of experience to be soaked up that the days feel huge, distended. Each hour of this time carries the same weight. In lessons as a young child, in days full of incident and peaks of concentration, time is like this: by the evening, the morning has become distant and remote, as if in a previous age. So much has happened. Is it possible that it can still be the same day? The same self? This is not like working time, narrowed by pace and necessity. It is not like holiday time, subject to novelty and schedule, to accommodating the plans of others. This is extreme time, heavy time. Pilgrimage time.

When I look back for the details of this day, the only item in my pocket notebook will be the address of the Princess Alexandra Hospital in Harlow. Until this point, I've crammed those small pages with the minutiae of observations, writing as I walk. Not this day. On this day, there is no room for reflection, no space to both hold a pencil and hold myself upright. Every step requires scalpel-blade concentration.

Still wrapped in my damp towel, I phone my oldest friend, my companion since the first day of our first school. Rosie is a great walker; she has spent weeks trekking in the Alps and regularly tramps around the Peak District. She lives a few miles away; she is expecting an update on my progress and the possibility of a stolen meeting. It's Friday evening, perfect timing for an end-of-the-working-week drink in a shady pub garden. When I phone her, she thinks it is to decide on a good place for supper. Instead, she finds herself on a rescue mission.

❖

It's foot Friday in A&E: wheelchairs, broken toes, crutches – and me. There is no dignity in the slow festering of a self-inflicted infection. Rosie props me up as we stand in line at reception. Her partner Michael comes in from parking the car and rushes off to find us water. I am fighting tears of disappointment, of fury with myself and of gratitude for these remarkable people who will do everything in their power to fix me, patch me up, keep me safe.

Ahead of us in the queue is a beautiful young woman in a wheelchair, pushed by her equally beautiful sister, the picture of grace under pressure. There's a longhaired, footballing youth with his parents, all glowing tan and flip flops, nursing the triumph of a sporting injury. There's a man with his arm in a bloodied sling, and his laughing friend who takes great pleasure in telling us all, in singing broken English, that the injured man was only supposed to be making dinner, not chopping up himself. They are all genial, accepting, gracious. Are they, like me, gibbering and railing on the inside?

The doctor gives it to me straight. She doesn't wince when she sees what I've been walking on. The infection will take at least 72 hours to respond fully to treatment. I am not to walk on it until it is completely healed, which could be a couple of weeks. There is absolutely no question of long distance walking any time soon. She narrows her eyes at me. 'Absolutely none.' Closed shoes are to be avoided at all costs. No covering with plasters or bandages; not even a gauze. 'Foot up, antibiotics and rest, and that's all.'

It is over. End of adventure. I have screwed it up. I have been forced to rely on others. I am incompetent. I cannot even propel myself on my own legs without doing terrible damage. If I were a medieval pilgrim, I would be a laughing stock. My foot would be gangrenous. I would, pending a miracle, be dead within a week.

Rosie and Michael take me back to the B&B to return the key, where the hosts are solicitous and the terrier expresses concern. My friends will not leave me here, however comfortable it is: they take me to their flat to minister to me, to make me laugh, to watch over me and feed me with takeaway curry.

That night, lying on the airbed on their floor, my foot raised up on pillows, I read 'The Legend of the Miraculous Cross of Waltham' adapted from a 12th-century account. A canon of Waltham Abbey recalls how, in his youth, a man called Matheus lived in the town. Matheus had an ulcerated right foot 'which was consumed…up to the ankle', becoming 'terribly and increasingly painful.' Preparing for his death, Matheus' mother and sisters pray for his soul before the holy cross of Waltham. That night, Matheus is visited by a dream in which the figure of Christ from the Waltham cross wrenches off his right foot, covering the stump in new skin. All pain is removed. In the morning, Matheus wakes to find his foot completely healed. The town rejoices, the bells are rung. The cross has worked another miracle.

❖

In the morning, strong antibiotics are going about their own miraculous, microbial duties on my right foot. The woozy fog that I had been peering through, that I had been in such denial about, has lifted overnight. Michael makes me coffee and stands by the fridge, eating a bowl of cereal, while I tell him of the amusing coincidence of the legendary right foot. I tell him about the blessing of the Waltham Abbey volunteer, the only one I've heard on this strange adventure. Michael is a Catholic. We speak in low voices of chance and happenstance. I am not credulous, but I am curious.

Has Waltham prevented me from further harm? The town kept me in its sights, bringing me back to notice it, to look again, to linger. It held on to my belongings and stopped me from walking the rest of those fifteen miles. The station of Waltham Cross delivered me to Ware. Ware delivered me to my friends. My friends delivered me to A&E.

The map in that folder is for a walking route that now, I cannot take. I no longer have need of that map. Waltham has seen to that.

If I get to Walsingham now, it will be on wheels.

'Mysterious ways,' agrees Michael, and heads out for his morning run.

❖

Pilgrims crawl into shrines, kissing surfaces, chipping off bits of tomb, gathering dust from crevices to stir into healing drinks. Bestowing ex voto offerings in the shape of infected or broken limbs: a wax hand, a tin heart. A lead foot.

I could crawl to Walsingham. I could drag myself on crutches. But I won't. Time is always the obstacle: not the humiliation, but the endless press of time.

Feet are fallible; lumps of bone and gristle and skin that are subjected to endless wear. Constantly depended upon, we mistreat them daily and rarely indulge or compensate them. I cannot be the first pilgrim to be undone in this way: foot injuries must have loomed large for the medieval pilgrim too. Outside the West door of the Abbey church of Iona, on that remote and holy Scottish Isle, is a shallow stone trough of miraculous properties. According to Argyll's inventory of monuments, the trough is known locally as 'the cradle of the north wind' and is credited with the property of attracting favourable conditions for travel. Pilgrims would wash their feet here, their soles pressing against the chiselled cross in the basin's base, presumably to cleanse themselves before entering the church, or perhaps to bear with them some drops of lucky weather-water before sailing home.

Mark Hall, a researcher at Perth Museum and Art Gallery, is fascinated by the role of feet in pilgrimage and has tried to locate pilgrims' footbaths elsewhere. Another stone basin of similar design – complete with an incised cross – has been found on the monastic island of Inishmurray in County Sligo, Ireland. Could this also be a place for ceremonial foot-washing? Hall thinks so. Are there more of these to be found? Were there pilgrims' footbaths at the holy sites of England too? Perhaps, Hall says, although they have yet to come to light. Such portable objects would be easy to remove and repurpose, making them likely targets of breakage and reuse at the Reformation. Such stone is too good to be left lying around on neglected abbey doorsteps. There may be sacred basins blocked into walls or buried in foundations; tangled in the briary hedgerows of fields after service as cattle troughs; gravel-lined and resting in the overgrown corners of gardens, reduced to birdbaths. Walsingham is known for its miraculous well water – could the shrine have housed a pilgrims' footbath? Hall thinks it likely that in places where full body immersion was possible, such as at the sites of holy wells, the humble footbath may have been superfluous.

For Hall, feet are a way into understanding pilgrimage. Feet have a cultural resonance. Think of all those toes venerated as relics. East Kent alone has boasted Augustine's footprint in a slab at Richborough's lost Saxon church, and Becket's shoe at the Harbledown well. Saints, angels and devils have left their treads to be preserved like trace fossils. Feet may, Hall thinks, be central to pagan pilgrimage in classical times too. He feels that there may be further examples of pilgrims' footbaths in the Near East, influenced by the washing of feet in New Testament passages.

But the straight answer for me, and the mess of my foot, is a simple halt. There are no holy blister-cures to be found on this route: no fair weather promises, no sacred ablutions. There is only rest, and the invisible wonder of Flucloxacillin.

A car journey to Cambridge station. A train ride to Ely station. A taxi to my parents' house and childhood home. An excruciating hobble over gravel to find the hidden side-door key, emergency access in their absence, let myself in and level onto the sofa. I have surrendered a portion of the pilgrimage, the Ware to Ely link, but here I can rest, muster myself, regroup.

I am in stasis. I cannot go on: I cannot go home.

A hiatus. Days wash in and out. My foot is elevated, seeping, throbbing. Time, precious and trickling away, becomes soupy with lack of movement. My parents come back early from their holiday to tend to me, admonish me, listen to my traveller's tales. I delay cancelling stops until the last, willing the foot back into wholeness, desperate to recover plans. But there is no undoing what is done. I have to swallow my defeat and wait, wait, wait.

❖

Day thirteen of pilgrimage is my first escape from the house, a brief venture back into the world, both feet in contact with the earth. Baby steps, rocking from the heel. Ely Cathedral – the shrine of Etheldreda, the end of the route for many past pilgrims – is almost on the doorstep, and about as far as I can manage. I will make it to this stop at least.

Extensive repairs are underway on the cathedral, the flank of the building Christo-wrapped. Romanesque beasts guard the top arch of the south door-within-a-door, jealous as dragons. I limp over to the site of Etheldreda's shrine, another Reformation victim, now reduced to an engraved slate set into the floor. Stout pillar candles mark the spot. Ely is a testament of wreckage and repair, the ebb and wash of history's fashions breaking and reshaping its banks. The leavings of iconoclast beheadings can still be seen in The Lady Chapel, although several animals have avoided the chop. The Millennium Mary statue is matronly and muscular, her depiction causing a local stir. She looks like a fitting martyr to me: this is a woman who has toiled in fields and will gladly get her hands dirty.

Evening prayer is in the central nave's choir stalls tonight, each seat panniered with carved reredos. On one side, the cowled head of a solemn pug-like man, tusked and bearded; on the other, a crouching grotesque with a finger in his mouth. A barn owl misericord under the seat. The craftsmanship of this space is astonishing, the figures both celebratory and irreverent. It's impossible to resist tickling a sainted ox under the chin or stroking the wooden plumes of a peacock. *Whoso hath a proud look and a high stomach, I will not suffer him.* The service includes a biblical reading full of botanical references amongst foliate carvings. Cypresses and cedars. I am the vine and you are the branches. Prayers ask that those involved in Brexit negotiations be 'imbued with wisdom'. After hours, the incense holders jostle for space in the verger's broom cupboard, litres of Waitrose Essential oil on the shelves amongst the votive candles.

I will get to Walsingham after all. Tomorrow, I will fast-forward to the Slipper Chapel at Houghton St Giles. This route, my planned leg three, would be four long days on foot; sixty-six miles by Merrill's extended route. Now, it will be a sprint in the car with my parents.

❖

Ely, Queen Adelaide, Shippea Hill, Burnt Fen. I tick them off my internalised schedule as we career past. Bleak high banks marking the arteries of dykes, the perpetual feeding and draining of fields. Celery and potatoes. Sugar beet. Acres of short-stemmed oats spreading like butter over black bread. Inside this hurtling shell of upholstered steel the roads feel closed to pedestrians, impassable. It would be ludicrous to walk these spaces, to risk the flash and compress of collision. Who would dare? Why?

We pass the RAF bases of Mildenhall and Lakenheath, my parents and I, they up front disagreeing about routes, me in the rear seat, leg outstretched. Clutching my notebook, staring out of the window, disbelieving. Such speed! Such blurring of sight! Air fields, high fencing, a funeral hearse at the church. The cottages here are flint and cobble. There's a noticeable increase in trees: evergreen leaking from the perimeter of Thetford Forest, willows leaning away from the wind across unbroken fields. A church in the middle of nowhere. A city for pigs. The ground is parched, the fallen pine needles a wildfire waiting to happen. Rusty fat hen is swollen with seeds. Bracken and fern curl in the heat, flares of yellow, brown and mauve under the trees.

Walking is the pace of attention. Riding in a car is like viewing the world through a speeding tracking shot. Sites and scenes flit by in a continuous dumb show: Brandon with its bungalows, brown 1970s boxes, adjacent pubs and the steep, slated church tower. School pick-up traffic crawling towards the crossroads. A stuffed giraffe in a florist's window. The Little Ouse. Signs for Weeting Castle and Grimes Graves. The long straight road north to Swaffham.

We stop at Swaffham for drinks, where six female mallards walk a determined single file to The Greyhound for table scraps. I shepherd them away from the wheels of a reversing car. The pavements of Swaffham are a lull, a temporary reassurance beneath my feet, but we're soon on the last length of road to Walsingham. Castle Acre is just a basin of grey ruins, spotted on a rise between trees. Weasenham, Tofftrees and Fakenham – places that I would have taken my time over and dwelt in – are momentary flashes of stone, brick and broken skyline.

Then the landscape opens out, a transom between high shaggy hedgerows across rolling arable fields. Dutch gables, St Giles Church, Houghton Le Dale milestone; a little cottage on a high bank; a signpost for The Holy Mile. This is it: this is the place. From here, I will finish my pilgrimage on foot. In a day dominated by tarmac and wheels, the sudden rash of pedestrians with their day packs are an incongruous, refreshing sight, and I long – with the longing of distance sharpened by separation – to be one of them. We pull into the car park. We have arrived at the final wayside resting place en route to Walsingham: the Slipper Chapel, the slype, the place between.

❖

Swifts are nesting in the toilets on site: one muddy-edged nest blocks the convex viewer of a security camera. Wood pigeons glean sandwich crumbs from the small marquee in the grounds. I track down the key for my shepherd's hut – a quaint narrow space with a bed, crucifix, fold-out table and kettle – and offload my kit. My parents inspect the facilities, insist on stocking me up with groceries, and announcing they will return rather than let me gamble on rural weekend buses, take their leave. When they are gone, I make myself tea in the only container I can find: a soup bowl.

Sheep and horses are grazing in the meadow next to the hut. A huge grey heron watches a stretch of reeds by a low-lying pond. After the automated whirr of the road, the quality of noise here is balm-sweet. Moorhens pip-pip past. Mayflies hum spirals against the window glass, flicking their long tails like ribbon dancers. A hare appears, running along the front of the far hedge. It stops in line with the hut and stretches to smell the air. Does it detect the presence of a watcher? If so, it doesn't mind the attention, taking its time scratching and combing out those long, black-fringed ears. It's the size of small cat crouching in the undergrowth, and equally unobtrusive.

We sit together, the hare and I, as the sun goes down. The hare nips at the tips of a dark patch of grasses, camouflaged against the long brown stalks. Swifts squeak and wheel, feeding in mid-flight. A klaxon of geese pass overhead and we both look up to see them, the hare and I, cutting their v-formation across the fading light.

As I look back, the hare bolts into sudden darkness and is gone, a ghost glimpsed in the gloaming.

❖

Mary is surrounded by lilies and gladioli. She's holding her child of course, who sits up, straight-backed and diligent, blessing and protecting her with one hand. It's quiet in the chapel, as directed by the 'please respect the silence of the shrine' signage – just a low electrical hum and the business of birds outside.

The Slipper Chapel was visited by a devout young Henry VIII and later desecrated on his command. Restored to the Catholic Church after centuries of neglect, including a period as a cow shed and barn, it is back in active use. I have the site to myself first thing, before the visitors and cleaners and daily duties of observance begin.

In the magic morning hour of early sun, sparrow song and dew-sodden surfaces, I shamble about, in flip-flops and fleece, reading all the signage I can find. A potted history of the chapel and its restoration, from cow shed back to centre of pilgrimage, is reproduced on boards in the car park. I read the text of the Walsingham Ballad, printed by Richard Pynson in the 15th century, praising the site as 'England's Nazareth' and encouraging pilgrims to visit. The grounds host a semi-circular Way of the Cross, the stations punctuated with life-size timber reproductions carried to the site in the great pilgrimage of 1948. In front of these is the new basilica, The Chapel of Reconciliation, mulberry brick with windows like arrow-slits faced with bottle-thick glass. All of the buildings are locked overnight, but by the time I've washed and had a makeshift breakfast, someone has done the rounds with keys and I can explore inside.

Beside the Slipper Chapel itself, smelling of stone dust and stale incense and the fresh hit of those lilies, is the Holy Ghost Chapel, housing a cabinet of curiosities – locket-sized reliquaries holding fragments from St Peter to John Paul II. It's impossible to tell what's inside, but the settings for these unseen jewels are exquisite. On another wall is a fragment of Mary's veil. It could be there, clasped inside all that precious filigree: or it could not.

With a couple of inches of padding and some loose lacing, and in the teeth of medical advice, I can now get my foot back in a shoe. I can make the final walk to Little Walsingham as planned. The going is still slower than usual, but the action of walking is almost perfect, the swing of leg and arc of heel moving like recalibrated pistons. A steward at the chapel advises me to stay off the road and walk the old railway line to the village, rather than risking the Holy Mile itself. I realise how sound this advice is when a truck speeds past on the road before the footpath, leaving only inches of verge.

The walk itself is edgeland perfection. There are linnets in the hedge, the banks of tall grasses tangled with cow parsley, pompoms of red clover and downy thistle clocks. The dull purple olives of sloes and flat cheeses of hawthorn are already starting to form. Miniature green fruits hang, full of slow-ripening promise, from a walnut tree. Below, a field is set aside for receiving pilgrims by the coachload, with his-and-hers pink-and-blue portaloos, a rank of wheelie bins and the shrapnel of multiple visitations: a shattered polystyrene cup, labels from water bottles, biscuit wrappers and shards of plastic cutlery. Further on, small espaliered trees along the road have the look of crosses, a sinister lining of the way.

Old Blind Dick's Lane. Back Lane. The first glimpse of medieval ruins, of bonding courses and pitched walls. The triple chimneys of a still-grand but crumbling house. The rustic toffee-tin perfection of pink rambling roses around a cottage door. The new Catholic church with its rotunda, air thick with incense, where I stop to light a candle of thanks for Michael. The bare-ruin'd choirs of the priory, now a centre for visitors again, but not long since a romantic backdrop in a palatial pleasure garden.

I am here: I made it. Somewhere nearby, a peal of bells sounds out a flat rendition of three of the seven joys of Mary.

❖

I stand by the last empty arch of the abbey, a potent symbol of damage and loss. Reformation destruction was especially brutal here, a determined stamping out of that 'witch of Walsingham', a female figure whose role in the Christian story had surpassed that of immaculate child-bearer. Mary had become a powerful intercessor in her own right: a saint, a holy queen. While theologians debated the problematic question of the virgin mother's womb, relic-sellers peddled phials of her breastmilk to credulous pilgrims. Erasmus wrote a satire about it. Falsingham, the Lollards called it. But however out of hand the cult of Mary became, however tacky the trinkets or dubious the dates or hokey the claims, what remains here speaks of violent intolerance. Every scene is a sign. The parched grass reveals the tell-tale outlines of the lost Holy House, the original shrine of Our Lady of Walsingham. The result of a visitation by Mary to the devout Lady Richeldis, the shrine – so say Pynson's ballad and the legend in the visitor's leaflet – was constructed by angelic hands overnight to stand as a replica of the holy family's home. Razed almost as rapidly by the Reformation, its skeleton is indelible nearly five hundred years on. It will not be ignored. Even the lightning-struck tree beside the gaping arch has splintered into a crown of thorns. As the contemporaneous ballad 'A Lament for Our Lady's Shrine at Walsingham' put it: 'Bitter, bitter, O, to behold / The grass to grow / Where the walls of Walsingham / So stately did show.'

Little Walsingham is postcard-perfect in places, tatty and in need of love elsewhere. It hits the sweet spot of the English village: the closed-down chip shop and empty restaurant, the wisteria-iced cottages and red-tiled roofs. Broken windowsills. A charity shop. A redundant railway line. Statues and Walsingham tea towels; incense cones and rosary beads; pewter pilgrim badges and aspirational bookmarks. A place held together by absences, a tourism celebrating the unseeable and unknowable. It is larger than I remember, my recollection of the village distilled into an essence rather than shapes or details. I experience a mild echo of that first feeling, that weird hum, standing in the central Common Place. My sense of the place is overlaid with exhaustion and expectation, with a now-trained eye for cataloguing specifics, and a peripheral awareness of other people going about their business; but nonetheless, I am completely smitten.

The Anglican shrine is on a separate site to the abbey ruins, just across and down the street. A blackbird sings inside the octagonal lantern tower of All Souls Chapel, filling the glasshouse space with sound. Next door is the Holy House shrine, a replica based on the footprint of the Richeldis original. The site of this new shrine was rededicated and expanded in the 1930s, on the cusp of World War II, a time when many would have felt the need for a miracle.

Inside, the Holy House radiates warmth from walls of candles. The Madonna at the centre of these lights, with her white veil, spread embroidered train and oversized crown, sits on a throne with shining scallop shell surround. Her garments are green and gold. The room is heavy with incense and hot wax. The votive candles flicker in their red and blue holders with a Calor-Gas heat. The altar is gold, gold, gold and silver.

And I have a moment of pivoting away towards the Reformation camp. A distant Puritan gene stamps an incredulous foot. Are there adults, it cries, that bow down before this idol and genuinely believe in its sanctity? Are there rational beings, it sneers, that are taken in by praying to this puppet? I find myself agreeing, for a moment, with Erasmus. The statue of Mary looks suspiciously like the result of a small child playing dress-up with dolls.

The crowds come in; a bell rings; the moment passes. I

have no trouble blaming Henry VIII for the cynical character of the English – our distrust of ritual, our lip-curling fear of being duped. Lapsed and animistic as I may be, I am determined to give Walsingham a fair chance. I have partaken in some dubious neo-pagan gatherings, danced in circles around bonfires and channelled invisible elements into objects. I have sung to the moon, lit ceremonial candles and attempted psychic group healing. I have meditated in a car park, for what it's worth. I'm game.

I take a seat at the back as a congregation steadily fills the nave. There's a sense of expectation so concentrated it could be canned. A priest sitting among us looks around, wrings his hands and hurries outside. Has he gone to remind someone in the vestry that they are 'on'? He returns a few minutes later and retakes his seat, watching the aisle and biting at the nails of his right hand.

He needn't worry. A presiding priest appears in a cloud of white vestments and begins the service of the 'Sprinkling'. We listen to a sermon about hosepipe bans, drought, and Psalm 63. 'My soul thirsteth for thee, my flesh longeth for thee in a dry and thirsty land, where no water is.' Then we file down the steps of the well for a ladleful of holy water from a plastic bucket, decking underfoot to prevent slippage. The water is warm, mineral and vaguely metallic, and as I receive a blessing I'm distracted by the thought of how many mouths have already met this ladle-lip.

After the service I explore the corner shrines and paraphernalia, walk around the gardens and take in the outdoor altar under its gazebo-style canopy. The site is tidy, with neatly-trimmed borders, broad paths and seats dotted near scented flowerbeds, a mix of forthright practicality and thoughtful concessions. I turn a corner and see a woman who was seated in front of me at the service, leaning against a wall, retching violently, a companion rubbing her back as she loses her share of holy well water. I look away and hurry past – perhaps the fewer the witnesses, the more hope remains. It's a blunt reminder that some still come here as desperate pilgrims, seeking a miraculous cure. Compared to such raw need, the purpose of my visit feels flimsy, whimsical.

I could spend several days shopping around the religious offerings of Walsingham. Aside from the Anglican shrine there are local parish churches. The Catholic church supplements the Slipper Chapel. There's a dark, icon-lined Greek Orthodox chapel in the old railway station, and a Russian church in Great Walsingham, just along the road. I take them all in, covering six miles altogether in my padded shoe. As I walk back from Great Walsingham across a field, two piebald ponies watch my approach with disconcerting interest. But it isn't me they are staring at – there's a crash and swoop just above me and a buzzard drops into the grass ahead, picks up a rabbit and beats hard to lift off again. The rabbit twitches, the buzzard loses its grip at take-off and the rabbit falls, hits the ground running, shooting into a bramble thicket. It only takes a couple of seconds and as I stand there, dumbstruck, processing the action, the buzzard lands in the branches of a tree across the field. It shouts with indignation, a screech like a rusted, angry gate-hinge. The horses watch the bramble patch with tangible respect. I keep an eye on the buzzard as I exit the field, reminding myself not to limp. That bird is massive.

The footpath back to the Slipper Chapel is busy with traffic now: joggers, strolling families, dog walkers. A young Franciscan in robes, trainers and 'Assisi' baseball cap nods as we pass. As I arrive, the local children are rehearsing a play for performance at the Grandparents' Pilgrimage Day. A chorus of wood pigeons thrums in the cloister garden. The sounds of an organ carry across the car park from the basilica.

It's odd to think of packing up and leaving, but I return home tomorrow. I wash out my clothes for the last time, hanging my T-shirt on the sole hanger from the window hook. I lay out my assortment of relics: bingo numbers, feathers, a penny and a button, a leaflet, a postcard, an ear of barley and a finger of rapeseed. I need to find a suitable reliquary for these treasures.

The shepherd's hut feels familiar already, a skin. The water meadow with its pipping moorhens, long lines of tiptoeing sheep and statuary grey heron is my back garden. A wren shuttlecocks in and out of the open door of the hut, lands on the fence outside to look in, then whirs in and out again.

Bonfire smoke and sheep dung on the breeze. The tear and chomp of grazing. The bobbing strut of a lone cock-pheasant, tail feathers peacock-bright against the low sunlight.

Do I feel like a pilgrim at journey's end? I'm not sure. Maybe I won't know how I feel until I complete that final stage of pilgrimage, return home and attempt to reassimilate. My triumph at being here is tarnished by the sense that I didn't earn my place, not fully. Like the Palmer in John Heywood's play, *The Four Ps*, I submitted to the 'dayly payne' of the penitent on foot; but when it got too much I copped out with modern medicines and conveniences. Am I missing something vital? If I had made it on foot all the way, the formula would be complete. Would that feel so different? Perhaps. I do feel enriched, even so.

I have noticed, discovered; experienced places keenly. The shrines of Walsingham are splendid and clearly meaningful, but for me, the old pump in the Common Place is a centre of power: a gathering place of forgotten pageantry and trade and gossip, the hub where the spokes of the lanes converge, radiating towards the ruined abbey, the Holy House, the shrines and churches and chapels. The Greek Orthodox chapel is a modest conversion in a single room, but it holds the stillness and weight of any cathedral. As James Harpur puts it, modern shrines may lack the aesthetic of ancient sites, but the presence of pilgrims and candlelight can 'create a powerful sense of the numinous'.

I am not converted, but I believe even more firmly in the glory of the everyday: now, at this moment, watching this field; or looking out across the Thames valley, with traffic roaring behind me. Even sitting in a pub garden with the cold stem of a glass at one hand, fingertips resting on the rough woodgrain of a picnic table. The miraculous familiar. Casual moments of synchronicity and serendipity; oases of kindness and miraculous rescues. Thin places to be sought and found, or happened upon.

As night comes on, the cooling wood of the hut creaks and settles. I look up from my final notes of the trip and spot the hare from last night. Was it watching me? It leaps up and disappears through a gap in the hedge.

I cannot draw the curtain: it feels like the end of something. At least I know that the hare is out there, somewhere. I sit, still as I can, until the darkness is complete: if I peer very closely, and remain patient, I might just make out the flick of a black-tipped ear.

The Return

hymn

to the fox scat

to the broken willow bough

to the horsefly

to the tart trick of unripe blackberry

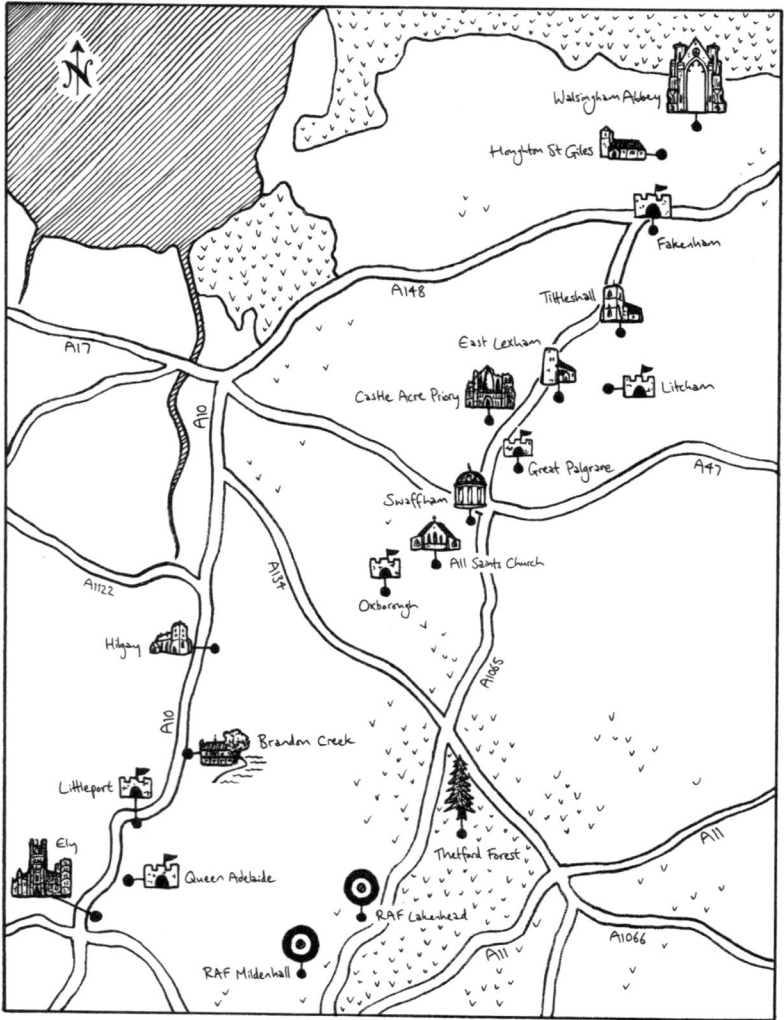

WALTHAM ABBEY DOESN'T LET GO. In the vestry of the abbey church is my map case with that itinerary and Merrill guide, an OS map and doom painting postcard, the miraculous tale of the foot-healing cross. It's November before I can get back, this time with my husband and son, and not on foot. Pulling up into the car park feels like cheating, but I'm back in ordinary time now, not pilgrimage time, and life is playing out against the clock.

Someone has left painted pebbles in the walls of the cloister entrance, fragments of text and images left for the curious, posted into little pockets of ruin. Balancing on edges. This is stealth advertising for the local judo club, but it's also a treasure hunt for those with keen eyes. My son gathers and replaces dozens of these smooth stones, delighted that someone has gone to such effort. As he posts a pebble back in its socket, I spot something moving at the foot of a wall, a glimpse of black tugging the ground. It's an enormous bumblebee, trapped in a slick of cobweb. The spider that laid this trap is at one end, hauling in its prey; at the other, the bee lifts and tugs at its tangled wing and back. I know the spider needs to eat, but I cannot leave it like this. I cannot unsee the attack. I find a stick and cut through the threads of web, separating predator and prey. The bee's wing and back are quick to clear, but it takes an age to extricate the rear right foot from the string of web, wrapped around it like candy floss. I lift away the last sticky filaments tethering it to the ground: the bee lifts, bounces and, after a few bumps, takes flight.

I feel the ghost tug in my own right foot behind the church itself, and the tree-shaded spot where I wrapped, unwrapped and rewrapped my injuries, still in denial about the extent of the damage. We greet the Harold Stone and my son poses for a solemn photo. This time the stone is decorated with floral tributes fading to brown, left behind by Harold fans from Sussex. Another pilgrimage of sorts.

Inside the church, a recorded voice reads the names of the fallen from the Great War. It's the Armistice Day centenary: the eleventh day of the eleventh month, a whole century on. The chapel gift shop is closed, so there's no access to the Doom Painting. We press ourselves against the glass like window-shoppers. A priest lets herself in and out of the door with shopping bags and, seeing our faces, allows us in to look at the mural. She laughs about redirecting visiting school groups away from the prodding devils and troublesome theology of Judgement to the stained glass nativity scene nearby. I ask about my lost package as she locks the glass door behind us: yes, it's in the vestry, and the verger will have it. A moment later the verger appears, balancing a pile of folders and a mug of thin white soup. He has the map case. I have the map case. Mission complete.

There's a mosaic built into the ground of Sun Street, marking the spot where the Greenwich Meridian line runs through the town. A blue Meridian gate in the abbey gardens, decorated with sun, moon and stars. A 14th-century abbey gatehouse and bridge. I missed them all in the fog of walking through pain, but here they are.

When I open the map case, it reeks of sunscreen and disinfectant.

❖

The air is swollen with the threat of rain. Clouds are thick, grey-blotted, over Canterbury West Station.

It's July, exactly a year since I first set out on my pilgrimage and walked from Canterbury to Faversham. This year's medieval pageant involved the same penitent Henry II, the same Queen Eleanor still giving him a piece of her mind. Beckett's ghost leapt with her ribbons. Schoolchildren performed a dumb show of the martyr's death. The procession bounced along in the heat: giants, horses, musicians and knights.

We finished in the public gardens with a Court of Love set to music, struggling to hear our cues from the singers and keep time with the brass section up on the grass rise. Canvas tents dotted along the riverside; small children seeking stamps for their medieval trail cards. Now I've changed out of my medieval garb and here I am again, walking shoes and backpack, a train ticket to Ely.

The last year has been eaten by the gentle worm of self-recrimination. I didn't finish. I didn't make it all the way. I can accept skipping the self-assembled section of Waltham to Ely, a bit of route-making DIY that didn't pay off. There were no major sites that I wanted to reach on the way, no ancient paths that I wanted to tread. That part doesn't matter so much. The piece of the puzzle that I do need to fit in, the missing link in my pilgrimage chain, is the elusive leg three, the walk from Ely to Walsingham. I want to earn my entry to the shrine. I want to remind myself that I can make this sluggish writer's body move. I am going to make it, lame or otherwise, on my own feet. I am propelling myself into a second pilgrimage, because without doing so, I will never have really completed my task, and so I cannot fully return.

And I have the pilgrimage bug.

It feels like no time, yet it's another world. My son has just turned ten. My soft, desk-bound body feels even more unfit and underprepared than last time. I have packed for fewer days on the road, yet my backpack feels heavier. And when I last made it to Ely, limping from train to taxi to resting place, I returned to the house I grew up in. Since then, my parents have moved into a flat in a retirement complex.

In the last year, my mother has been through numerous operations and hospital stays. Yesterday, tests revealed another lump. What this signifies remains to be seen, but it's an opportune time to visit. With the latest concerns over my mother's health and my father's birthday next week, this lining up of dates feels like irrefutable synchronicity. Waiting on the station platform, boarding the train, shoving my pack into the skinny rack above a seat, I have a nagging, superstitious inkling that I should seek some kind of intercession at the shrines of Walsingham.

A storm gathers as the train starts to move. The passenger in the seat in front is liberal with an aerosol of sweet, fern-and-resin-scented deodorant. It hangs in cloying particles, strong enough to taste. Even from today's short procession, the soles of my feet are burning. It's clear that my son has only the vaguest understanding of what I am doing and why. He knows that the walk made me ill last time. But it's only fifty miles or so, I say, and it's not as hot as last year. I am walking this reprise of leg three in shorter sections. I will be staying in Ely for a couple of nights. All will be well.

There are many ways to Walsingham. After driving those roadside stretches through the fen, I've worked out a new route from Ely, another patchwork of old roads, footpaths and bits of John Merrill's London to Walsingham guide. The Fen River Way from Ely allows for most of a day's bankside walking. Then east towards Oxburgh Hall, far enough to get on the second day, but near enough to get a ride back to Ely for the night. Then Merrill's route from Cockley Cley to Castle Acre: a definite mark on the map for the medieval pilgrim, and a rare bed and breakfast stop. Finally, the road north to Fakenham and the Slipper Chapel.

I've booked into the shepherd's hut again. I picture the view across the water meadow, the stillness of the shrine site at night, the sound of sheep moving through long grass.

❖

Springhead Lane: the riverside walk. There are early playground visitors here, climbing, swinging and zip-wiring, ahead of the annual Aquafest. A group of trainee Lowland Rescuers cluster in their hi-vis jackets. Pleasure boats pass with a low motorised buzz. Rowers from the Cambridge Club lean and stroke as one. The footpath is pink-verged: thistles, umbelliferous wildflowers like rosy cow parsley, brambles with the fruit already setting. A pair of mute swans fly low over the water, wings beating like laundry in a high wind.

A small island in the river, intended as a haven for grebes, has been overtaken by nesting black-headed gulls. Dabchicks walk on the water near the tin-sided engineering workshop. Four coffee-and-cream bullocks, wide as sofas, stand guard in a side slip, herding passers-by towards a kissing gate and away. They stagger their numbers to create a wall, licking salt from each other's backs, flicking flies from each other's ears. Cuckoo Bridge is painted with a graffiti of guano; a forgotten fishing boat rots in a choke of lily pads.

I am not walking alone. Mum has announced that she's walking with me today, and Dad is seeing us across the river. We use the old iron bridge to cross to the far bank, towards the main road. The dilapidated bridge is surfaced with boards like old shed felt, the sides blocked in with fencing wire. Dad says that this bridge was an access route for workers to the sugar beet factory, built for purpose.

I have a vague memory of daredevil scootering across this bridge as a child, but it seems hard to believe. But then my parents' new flat looks over at the bungalow where my grandparents lived, which is harder yet to process. The path we took to the river was the one my grandfather, when he was still willing to get out of a chair, took me for walks along as a child: down to the railway bridge and back, naming plants, checking on the horse that put its neck over the five-bar gate, miraculously recognising the calls of unseen birds.

Dad waves us off and we step out together, my mother and I, swinging our arms in determination. I'm suspicious about the durability of Mum's summer footwear, but she insists that these are the comfiest shoes she possesses. Through the day we will take it in turns to play leader when the path narrows, walking two abreast whenever there is room. This is sociable walking, a ramble with mileage and attitude: chatting and observing, jotting down the occasional note. And in those lulls between speech, the rubber-soled sound of a second pair of footsteps will continue to beat time, marking out my mother's near and constant presence.

A sign to Littleport: four miles. Two rowing boats with women's eights pass in quick succession, the women rowing hard, a man bellowing at them through a megaphone from a raised tug behind. The footpath is a trench between waist-high nettle and thistle, impossible to follow. The road along the bank is the only way. A flock of juvenile geese scatter from the river's edge, gliding off in single file. They are followed by a single swan, clearly part of the flock, bringing up the rear like a governess chivvying her charges.

In Queen Adelaide the footpath returns, a shorn raised bank. The landscape rolls out, flat and low. Lime green beet tops in the field below are neon-bright against the black soil. Fen soil, a fine tilth: the darkest compost. Fruitcake-rich, coffee grounds-dark, blood-soaked and iron-laden.

❖

Every time I see the fens sweep out like this it gives me the same tightness in the chest, that ache of vastness. Some people get this from looking at mountains or a clear night sky. For me, it is that formidable call to the horizon: flat fields, wide open and coal black, or the sea, expansive and churning under a wet sky.

I fell out with a friend over this soil many years ago. The youngest son of an Irish Catholic family, born and raised in Cambridgeshire, he spent his late teens and early twenties working himself out. I should have had more patience, but at the time his arguments seemed needlessly polarised. The English were an ancient enemy he was forced to live amongst. So how did I fit with his imagined line of cruel overlords, stretching back centuries? He was reading a lot of Celtic Twilight literature. He told me that our difference was in the language of land. 'For the Irish, it is peat,' he said, on that heated coach journey. 'But the English talk about soil.' The inference was clear: soil is cultivated, used; peat is raw. I told him to stop talking bollocks, but he was right in literary terms. Englishness equals exploitation. To be Irish and to love peat is noble and holy; to be English and concerned with soil is to be unnatural and unjust. It was a political shorthand that I didn't understand, but I was offended on behalf of the landscape. My landscape. My friend was disparaging the soil of the fens. To me, that dark mysterious matter was utterly holy: from seabed to marshland to the stuff of ridge and furrow, it had been drained and worked, yes, but it had never lost its power, its deep-molasses magic. Its bleak and blasted witchcraft. I still feel the same. Never mind those stale metaphors of national identity and inheritance, so readily abused. Never mind the rhetoric of power and resistance. Why shouldn't I love fen soil the way another might love peat? Was that such a terrible love that I should hide it, feel ashamed?

Along the river are more rowers, isolated moored boats, solitary fishermen. Bees, damsel flies and miniature brown butterflies lift from the flowering clover underfoot. The pylons here are the shape of colossal goalposts, stapled into the horizon. We stop on a bench just outside Littleport, waving to boats, flexing our ankles. Mum grew up here. She recalls Sunday School outings to this stretch of river: to a farm perhaps, picnics or church teas.

There are swans in the river outside the Swan in the River pub. A row of anglers crouch in platforms cut into the bank. Riverside houses boast private moorings and hot tubs. There is money here now, as Mum points out: stables, paddocks, an exercise yard with gymkhana jumps. From the Littleport roundabout it's a long stretch of roadside walking, the bank thick with reeds and impassable on this side of the river. It means navigating the gnarling spoil of long grass and nettle clumps, ankle-twisting potholes and the usual highway hazards-in-waiting: crushed blades of Coke cans, man-traps of split and spiking plastic bottles, breakdown and crash-site leavings. Snarling curls of rusted wire. A massive straw bale takes up a chunk of sedge border, tipped from a swinging trailer and left to blacken with mildew in rain and sun. There is the ubiquitous single shoe. A mushroom farm with bricked up windows squats, secretive as a concrete bunker, by the roadside.

Some cars give a wide berth, but most of the walking here means side-stepping into an uneven camber whenever a vehicle passes. We point out the worst obstacles to each other, toe-stepping and twisting. Eventually the riverbank flattens, so we cross to walk a strimmed stretch. It widens out, pasture-like and even, until Brandon Creek. We stop in The Ship for lunch, making the most of a table in the sunshine, stretching our calf muscles. A family with a boat moored here fish from the bank, the teenage boy zipped into a black Puffa jacket despite the warmth. From here, it's another stretch of road before we can turn off to the quiet routes around Southery and Hilgay. At least there's a wider verge and cycle lane to act as an extra margin, and we are grateful for reduced side-stepping. A heat haze hangs over the road: it's hotter now, the sun on our necks casting squat shadows before us. When we do step into the grass to avoid passing trucks, crickets spark up like springing seeds, the rattle of their chorus audible above the roar of wheels.

The roadkill here is small: mostly felled aerial life struck mid-flight by speeding vehicles. Songbirds. Bumblebees. Numerous wasps. A pair of dragonflies, reduced to rusted husks in the sun. Further on, a flattened hedgehog in the road, spines glistening white on black. A pigeon with a detached wing flung aside in the grass.

Along the ferry bank road, the cycle lane becomes a separate raised way dotted with brazen splashes of poppies. Flat fields of crop stretch out: grains, flowering potatoes, the forget-me-not mist of flax. A lapwing wheels, pipes and settles by the edge of the field, posing for identification. A gap in high distant hedges reveals a great, majestic chestnut horse, standing as if at a picture window, watching the world.

It's a long fourteen miles – nearly fifteen, as we reckon it. Rather than risk Sunday closing at the village pub, we stick to the main road and head for the café of a garden centre. When we reach the counter, a young man tells us that we've just missed last orders, but looking us over, takes pity and allows us a bottle of juice apiece. Our drinks are gone in seconds.

There's nowhere to stay overnight out here, no pilgrim's almshouse or wayfarer's hostelry. Instead we'll return to Ely by car and I will pick up the route again tomorrow. As we wait for Dad to collect us and drive us back, we stretch out on the planks of a picnic bench, pressing our spines into the hard wood.

What does it mean to be walking again? Today, it is solely of the body. Step, step, step. Stumble. Sweat and dust. A companionable marathon. A Very Long Stroll. The walk of the determined after disaster: a place to get to. Lying in the shade, flattening my hips, raising and stretching my calves. Knots of knuckles testing and easing the dull aches of lower back.

Sitting up at last, I find the slippery backing of a strip of anti-blister tape in my pocket. It's my relic for the day. When I check my feet this evening, they will be perfectly preserved: soap-smooth, pink and blister-free.

❖

The riverside at Hilgay is pretty in an obvious way, but today the village is populated with barking dogs designed to see off strangers. After a short stretch of the A10 cycle path and verge, the rest of the route should be blissfully quiet. Traffic booms over the bridge above the Great Ouse Cut-Off, the water calm below, the sun reflecting moon-like and silver on the still surface.

The cool breeze, if it lasts, will make walking easier. Mum has decided to join me again today, although her right foot has rubbed to form blisters and she has resorted to 'comfy sandals'. I point out that we are aiming at fourteen miles again; maybe more, if we're to get as far as Cockley Cley. But if we don't manage it, I can make up the difference tomorrow. Even though we walked with light daypacks, we both have aching lower backs. Day two is always the hardest, I say, like some seasoned pro, bringing out the signs of shock after the adrenaline of beginning wears off.

Behind the sign for Fordham are the elaborate gates

of Snowre Hall, oak leaves and snarling boars' heads, a long English driveway between an avenue of young trees. A medieval settlement stood here, deserted through sickness or neglect. The hall is a patchwork, part medieval greathouse, extended over the centuries, the name on records swinging between Snowre and Snore. A last rallying place of Charles I, said to have held council here during the Civil War. Standing by those gates now, it seems like a dangerous place to meet: we're still in galloping distance of Ely, that Cromwellian lion's den.

Turning into Hilgay Road, the noise drops away. Here is the idyll of Norfolk country roads: broad fields full of bronzing crop, pasture, mixed woodland, occasional stacks of piled timber. Birdsong and faint stirrings in the undergrowth, a blossoming, foliate hedgerow. The only distraction, save for the odd car, is the proliferation of green 'Private Land' signage. No Public Access. Keep out. Entrances to vast fields of barley are blocked by monumental tree trunks.

These giant tree trunks are ideal to squat behind for a pee. I become a defiant fox marking new territory. Mum confesses that this is her first experience of open-air urinating – remarkable, given her many years of camping and foraging. She disappears, discrete, to a masked area of field margin.

Grey squirrels dart ahead and swing through the trees

beside us. Further on, a cache of collectors' cards has scattered along a stretch of hedge, dampened and thickening with dew. Lost from a car, perhaps? Sacrificed by a child in a fit of pique? I pick up the giant panda card, a relic for the day. Behind a paddock of horses is a chapel-like block of stone, an old barn or store. We endure the usual alarm-dog pursuit along the fenced perimeter.

There is further dog commotion as we approach the next name on the map, West Dereham. A terrier has escaped from one of the houses onto the road and will not go back to safety. The owner tells us about this as we pass, the terrier sniffing Mum's ankles before making another run for freedom. As neighbours corral the dog behind the house we become trapped by the owner's insistent mythmaking. He tells us that there is no centre to the village anymore, that the houses were burnt following an outbreak of plague in the 1670s, brought to the village by a city cloth merchant. He claims that the footpath running beside his house dates back to Vikings walking from Denver Sluice to Thetford forest. He regales us with tales of the threats he has made to parcel couriers, passing travellers and the gamekeepers of a nearby estate. We need to keep moving. Mum tries to extricate us with politeness. I try not to look at the man's pyjama bottoms and slippers. He talks on and on, his dog all but forgotten in the excitement of having a fresh, captive audience.

There may be no picturesque run of shops and cottages, but there is a village sign, a village church and a map of footpaths and cycle routes. None of these seem to connect to Denver, where the first sluice was built by a Dutch engineer as part of a great drainage project in the 17th century. And Thetford may be an ancient town but gives its name to a new forest, planted for timber about a century ago. Vikings? I don't think so. Still, it's easy to weave a story from this spot, with its little bridge, its tumbledown feel, its midpoint, just-passing-through mood. It's the kind of place where anything could have been. Where anything – or nothing – might happen.

After Flegg Green the idyll is over. The A134 means stepping into whips of long grass and rat-tail plantain to avoid dusty wind-baths from ploughing lorries. Roadkill litters the verge in varying degrees of desiccation. The grass hides patches of scarlet pimpernel and craters that jolt the hips. It's slow and treacherous. A buzzard glides and circles overhead, waiting for a truck to hit us.

We make it across to the Oxborough road. A peacock calls. New potatoes have dropped from a trailer, lining the route like a breadcrumb trail. From one stretch of hedgerow comes the lemon-drizzle punch of warm honeysuckle. A 'Frogs Crossing' sign heralds a sallow rise over green water, the surface alive with skimming bugs, but no sight or sound of amphibian life.

Are those grey shapes under the spreading trees deer? Or a mirage? Are those low flashes of sunlight the reflecting bonnets of parked cars? How much further? How much more?

It's a long, long road before the tease of the eagle-topped gates of Oxburgh Hall, and further still to get in: an enticing country pub on the corner, the car park, the visitor's entrance, the showing of National Trust passes.

Dad, now designated provisioner and punkah wallah, awaits us in the café with cold drinks. The hall itself is worth the walk, its heavy dignity a sobering smack in the face as we, leaden with bodily concerns, head straight for rest and refreshment. Stately right angles, elegant moat, intricate knot garden: all designed to humble, to reduce any right to grumbling stomachs or aching ankles, to the selfish demands of the footsore. It deserves respect and attention, but once we've eased our shoes off under the table, we both know we've seen enough for one day. Exhaustion draws its curtain. Cockley Cley can wait until tomorrow.

Bookshop. Gardens. Vegetable plot. All should hold our interest, but are seen through smog. Mum and I wear matching expressions of fatigue. Our feet roll. Our brains ache with sensory overload. We plonk down into garden chairs and watch other visitors enjoy the site. When we eventually drive away, I prickle with guilt for not exploring more – not looking at the church with its terracotta tombs, not visiting the priest-hole in the house… But I'm done. I'm beaten. I'm cashing in.

These two days feel very different to last year's journey alone. Is this what it's like to pilgrimage in a group? Or has this become a walking holiday, a sightseeing tour? It's convivial. There is much talking, which means less noticing perhaps, but also a shared sense of what is seen and passed through, a sounding board for observations. But it does not feel like psychogeography: I'm looking, and recording, but I'm not sensing those unseen vibrations of place.

Group dérives can be fruitful – indeed, the Situationists were keen on them – and it strikes me that for the practice to work, shared intention and expectation are therefore necessary. Mum and I are walking along the same route but in different ways. Is it pilgrimage, then? Harpur claims that the secular pilgrim 'can combine the roles of pilgrim, hiker and tourist at the same time'. Perhaps I am simply re-entering this third stage of pilgrimage, the part of the journey before immersion, from a different angle to last time. And if that eventual oneness with the landscape remains elusive, the journey is already reminding me, in brilliant flashes, of what it is to be outside and in the world – air on the skin, sun on the face, pollen itching the nose – instead of being chained to desk and computer screen, or breathing the recycled air of office and meeting room.

It's clear that Mum needs the outdoors too. This walk is proving something, perhaps, and we talk about how it's good to remind ourselves that we can make our bodies do things, even if they complain about it. Mum is used to the sprawling detached house that she and Dad built: its extension and garden room, the long lawn and flowerbeds, the hidden corner with its sheds, the fruit trees and horse chestnut, the old well with its pump. Living two floors up in an apartment is a challenge. 'I just want to be able to step outside,' she says. There are large windows and a skylight, and Mum has improvised a raised bed for salads in the kitchen, but there is no balcony or roof garden. I picture her flinging a window open and stepping out into air, hanging there like a figure in a tapestry, arms wide, to feel the breeze.

Back at the complex, the three of us drink tea at a table in the communal garden and reimagine the buildings with balconied platforms. Room for a few pots and a garden chair. I remove my shoes and socks, spread my bare feet out on the cool patio and marvel silently at my still pink, unblistered skin.

It cannot last. We only did ten or eleven miles today: I have sixteen miles to cover tomorrow to stay on schedule. Tonight I will sleep like the dead, pushing down dreams of never-ending tarmac.

❖

Sixteen miles to cover today. Seventeen miles tomorrow.

I'm getting there – checking off the distances, filling in the gap – but this walk isn't just about getting it done. There's some of that, certainly: a determination to complete, to assuage my feelings of failure. But I'm also longing to get back to the liberty of solo walking. It's time to feel like a wandering hermit again, stepping out on the unravelling ribbon-way of pilgrimage.

I wake in anticipation of two days of solitary and potentially tough walking. As soon as I'm up, Mum declares that she has made a decision – she will meet me tomorrow for the final stretch, and when we get to the Slipper Chapel, we'll all go somewhere for dinner. It's Dad's birthday today. If it wasn't, and they hadn't already made plans with friends, she'd be coming with me now.

It takes a few minutes to adjust to this: to erase the image I had of myself walking alone; arriving at Houghton St Giles, intrepid and limping; standing there in silence. Taking time at the chapel to process the walk: to reflect, to write. But I muster myself. The thought of Mum's impending hospital appointment hangs, the great unspoken, over everything. Today there is a lunch with friends – a double birthday celebration – after which Mum plans to buy some walking shoes. I suggest meeting them partway tomorrow, so that she doesn't attempt all seventeen miles in new shoes with existing blisters. It takes a little persuasion, but we reach agreement in the car to Oxborough. I don't want her to exhaust herself, but can't help admiring her grit. I hope I will prove as tough.

Hugs. Happy birthdays. Breakfast. A drive that stitches together the stopping places of the days before at incorporeal speed. By the crossroads at Oxborough I get out, shoulder my backpack and hit the road alone.

It has rained overnight, the air now tinged with a wet-straw-and-tea scent rising from the fields. The sky is a pale wash of blue and grey: the colour of jam jars full of milky paint and water after a school art class. Pigeons clatter in the tops of trees, loud enough to be harvesting coconuts. Solitary walking does this, tuning in the ears across increasing distances. Close to, thin twigs snap underfoot like firecrackers.

The shutters are open on a long-sided barn, emitting the squeals and stink of pigs. The roadside foliage shifts from lush hedgerow to pine trees. Traffic thins out. A Forestry Commission sign declares that the mass of trees here is the edge of Thetford Forest. The air is diffused: there is water nearby, hiding behind those trees.

❖

The church at Cockley Cley is a handsome, squat flint building with a collapsed Saxon tower, the tube of it broken open like a brandy snap. Three crosses are ranged over the roof and porch. It's too early for the pub next door, the wonderfully named Twenty Church Wardens, to be open. There are quaint cottages with climbing ivy, modern semis with satellite dishes. The village sign shows an enormous stag posing before the church, tower intact, and a plump pheasant by a stout, grain-laden wheatsheaf. This is shooting country. To one side of the village green, monumental gateposts herald an enormous driveway. The remains of a pigeon armageddon are strewn across the grass.

A woman clutching a canvas bag stands by the gates. She appears to be waiting for a bus, but the bus stop is on the other side of the green. A distant dog bark to the left, gun reports to the right: when I look again, the woman has disappeared. I keep moving, focusing on the prospect of a café stop in Swaffham. Turning the corner, I see the woman with the bag again, watching the road. There: gone: there again. Disappearing and resurfacing like crop marks in wet weather, like the leper hospital that once stood in this village but can no longer be found, only felt. Like the deer, or ghosts of deer, beneath the trees on Oxborough Road.

The rumble of occasional cars. Beyond the village, the spin-cycle racket of a combine harvester shudders into silence and the machine pauses mid-field. A woman passes on a shopping bike, a reassurance of nearby civilisation. The scent of lime blossom is a sudden nosegay on the path, the trees flanking another long driveway: Cockley Cley Hall. The estate must be vast. The blossoms are beyond tea-making, the flower heads still sweet but the centres ripening and swelling like green cloth buttons. I pick a piece of lime and put it in my pocket. If it survives the walk it could be today's relic. On last year's route into London, the lime blossom was already heaped in desiccating piles of leaf litter; that the flower heads are still on the trees this year proves that the weather is nothing like as fierce. Not yet, at least.

An invisible aircraft roars above, hidden by cloud. The harvester picks up the noise, buzzing into life, kicking out crop dust like smoke. A line of spruce trees arrays itself against the path, a Christmas market. One tree even has a red tag on it, marked as if sold.

I almost step on the great claw of a dismembered leg, grey and scaly. Probably pheasant, although there are no other clues or parts nearby. A couple of the pine trees here have limbs bent at right angles, as if designed for sitting and swinging on. As if intended for something to perch here, watching.

Across the road is a ploughed field. Around the edge of

the field, pushing at the boundaries, the forest presses in. It is dark and dense there, marginal, Peter-and-the-wolf territory, the trees and spaces in between still, but beckoning. The hairs on my arms begin to prickle. The forest groans and roars: those unseen aircraft noises are low enough to play acoustic games with cloud bank and treetops. That's all. But even so. Whether new forest or ancient woodland, the sweet, deep fear is the same. The sheer mass of mobbing shapes; the lure of shade and sap; the chill-thrill prospect of glimpsing the otherwise unseen. Forests are a ripe setting for encounters. What dwells in, or beneath, those trees? I could cross here and go in, leave the path and wander, surrender to atavistic imaginings. But no. Today, I must not digress. I stick to the path, tracing the chromatic hem of the forest, keeping it firmly on my left. I can't help peering in, hoping, and dreading, that something will be peering back.

❖

After the fairy tale promise of the forest is the playground of Swaffham golf course. Child-friendly mown turf, sand pits and flags, the toy-town clubhouse. White-haired golfers in nursery colours open and close the boots of shiny Tonka cars.

Swaffham feels rustic around the edges. The outlying estate has street names echoing Norfolk towns, the centre a rural theme-park feel, a picture-book litany of trades and places: Shoemaker's Lane, Orchard Place, The Paddocks care home. The church clock chimes twelve and the air smells of fresh laundry. The wind turbine waves a spiky dorsal fin over the roofline.

Market cross. Assembly rooms. I remember this spot from last year and hove straight for the coffee shop. The coffee here will be worth the walk. I order, remove my backpack, unlace my trainers and sink into a parasolled chair.

The world moves around me in its unhurried, Norfolk-market-town way. A deliveryman flirts with a waitress, the back-and-forth a well-practiced routine. A retired couple take the next table and discuss ways of cooking the fish they have bought for supper. A woman with a string bag full of vegetables stops to read a notice, leek tops tickling her wrist and a frilly cabbage squeezing obscenely against the diamond fishnet. I make the mistake of getting out my phone to send a reassuring text about my progress and am blasted by emails, one of which is so passively aggressive that it sucks all the joy out of my arrival. Why did I look? I need to cut that string. I curse, turn my phone over, sip the orange juice I was fantasising about back in Cockley Cley, and breathe, breathe, breathe.

About seven-and-a half miles down. Five to go. The breeze

is picking up and with it, the shallow-aired feel of coming rain.

Swaffham is a place of journeying and passing through, of joyful and expedient return. The legend of a local pedlar who found buried treasure here is commemorated by a roadside plaque. A dream told the pedlar to seek his fortune on London Bridge; he duly travelled to London, stood on the bridge, and waited for something to happen. Eventually a shopkeeper enquired what he was doing. On hearing the story of the pedlar's dream, the shopkeeper laughed that he too had dreamt of finding riches, buried in an orchard in some obscure town in Norfolk, but that he was not fool enough to waste his time making such a journey. The pedlar promptly returned to Swaffham, dug in the orchard behind his house and uncovered the treasure.

It's a charming fable of seeing the hidden value of familiar places, of treasuring what we already have. To journey forth and return home, richer for the experience. Today the space in front of the pedlar's plaque is closed off with cones; as I stand there, two workmen in yellow vests appear and paint fresh parking spaces on the tarmac, limning the grey surface of carpark with molten gold. My route continues out of town, through residential streets. The clock strikes one. A man clipping an overgrown hedge stands back to reveal a street name: Peddar's Grove. The Peddar's Way, that ancient wayfarer's route, begins with bungalows and hanging baskets, council houses, a Territorial Army training centre and the sound of revving motorbike engines. The wind turbine is a massive daisy that's been subjected to a game of *he loves me, he loves me not*. Then the way thins into a country track with hawthorn and bramble, fat hen and flowering mallows, cut through by the speeding lorries of the A47 and the turning blades of that turbine. There are no walkers here, no peddars or pedlars, just a grinning man in a mobility scooter coming the opposite way, flag flying behind, shopping basket in front.

No rain yet, despite the heavy air. The only moisture is the muck whipped up from the wheels of a passing tractor. A fingerpost sign at the turning for Palgrave Hall gives the details of the nearest GENERAL STORE, three quarters of a mile away, including the phone number. A sure sign of remoteness. The tractor turns into a field ahead, the sound of the driver's tuneless singing clear above the thunder of wheels and engine. It's a surprise to find a row of houses on this back lane – a prostrate man fixing his car in a front garden, a sign for a holistic therapist, washing on a line. A lost dog poster on a telegraph pole. After these signs of routine and habitation the way breaks down into a rough stone-and-sand path, grass pushing through in tough clumps, back into the beyond.

A meadow with the dancing ash of numerous butterflies. A

huddle of black sacks that morph into bullocks at the twitch of an ear. Waving crop, rolling fields, a wooded rise. A scene so bucolic it could feature on a war-time Pathé News report, stirring the patriotic pot. I want to shout out my delight: this is the treasure of walking, the payback for trudging those A-roads. It's now that I feel the start of that melting away, of a pilgrim surrendering to the landscape, shifting from observation towards a promising state of communion. Aside from the distant growl of farm machinery, the loudest sounds are the song of a blackbird and the buzz of proximal hoverfly wings.

The remains of Palgrave, a lost medieval village, are visible in the undulations of a field amongst straw bales, lime trees and a sunken pond, home to a pair of cruising mallards. How vast was this site? The wall enclosing adjacent farm buildings is a patchwork of stone held together by brick bonding courses. How much of the farm is built from repurposed dwellings? Arrow-tailed swifts dip in and out of the yard, rising to their nests in the barn eaves. An ancient hearthstone, a chipped Victorian brick, a loose corner of corrugated sheet metal – it's all the same to them. I pick three ears of barley from the roadside, flung so wide from the crop field that they must have been sown by birds.

Tarmac. A single car passing the signpost for Castle Acre – two-and-a-half miles via Peddar's Way. The grassy footpath runs behind a hedge, separate from the road and guarded by a felled tree. This stretch doesn't last long, but it's a marvel, a broad avenue lined with hedgerows. A ritual, processional space, a place apart and out of time, even with those pylons stepping away in the corner of the eye. Walking it, I notice a slight shift in my torso, the opening up of ribcage, the relaxing of shoulders. I'm sucking the air like candy here. I'm letting go.

Pine woods on the horizon. Across the broad A1065, handy roadworks regulating traffic flow. South Acre road. WARNING – SHOOTING MAY BE IN PROGRESS. A fleece of seed clocks tangle the ground, snowdrift on the verges. There's so much, but it's not clear where the heads have come from. Old Man's Beard? Thistledown? A tractor-width gap into a field reveals Castle Acre below, its church tower, priory site and toothy ruins. The sight of it is a joyful slap, enough to awaken any walker.

A sign warns of a ford ahead. At a grand farmhouse, a barn rings with the sounds of industrious carpentry, tools scattered on a workbench in the yard. And then the ford: a sudden stone-and-water mass at the end of the path. The water is clear and shallow, moving steadily to the left. The priory is clearly visible from the ford footbridge, the water running towards it. Even in ruin it elevates – a sweep and kick to the chest, a lightness to heavy feet. How must it have felt to medieval pilgrims on this way? A bed for the night, a meal, feet in the stream. Another step closer on the way to Walsingham.

A mayfly helicopters across the surface of the ford. It's tempting to put my feet in, but that would mean damp socks for the final mile. I throw in a grassy seed head, Pooh-stick style, and make a wish to be carried downstream. This is the River Nar. Looking at how clear it is – are those cresses midstream? – it must be good for fish in the deeper channels. A shape darts upstream, a minnow perhaps, too quick to be sure. It hides as my shadow nears.

I stop to examine what looks, at first, like another roadside shrine, but is actually a child's rainforest project. A shoebox diorama of collaged plants and facts about the Amazon; a plea for conservation. It's heartening that its young maker has faith in the power of this object to interest and move, to credit the lumbering world of careworn adulthood with a sense of mass responsibility. Heedless of eco grief, a local spider is making itself at home in the cardboard microhabitat.

❖

I arrive in Castle Acre village, my stop for the night. It's picture-pretty with an impressive church, tidy cottages, a Bailey Gate. A very welcome tearoom, still open, two tables on the narrow path in front, tea and scones and the easing off of boots.

I check into the Ostrich Inn. My room is downstairs, shady and chill, ivy tangling the back window. The slate-painted walls reflect the brewing sky outside. It's cellar-cold and damp in here, the light gloom-green as an old fish tank. A moustachioed cavalier watches from above the bed as I commit the summertime travesty of plugging in the heater. My bones ache. The bed calls. But it's too soon. After a shower and change, I take Merrill and my notebooks up to the bar and calculate distances over a gin and tonic.

There are several options for tomorrow's stretch, but time is limited. Should I follow Merrill to Litcham, Tittleshall, and find the fabled lost village of Pudding Norton? Merrill's church-sightseeing tour could clock up twenty miles, but trimming it down means giving in to more roadside walking. I flex my calves under the table: sixteen today, and I'm still in one piece. Seventeen feels doable. A shorter route via Rougham and Helhoughton would commit me to two miles of the A1065. But whatever way I go, there's no short option without roadside walking on the final stretch from Fakenham. I'm still undecided over pizza. I'm still undecided over a fat glass of wine.

In bed, the cavalier's stare is reflected in a mirror. 'Which way?' I ask. He frowns. I frown back.

I have no memory of switching out the light.

❖

There's no sign of the advertised eight-o'clock breakfast. The pub doors are locked and the lights out. Rain threatens. It's time to hit the road.

The early start means a perfect view of the castle, rising above a rain-and-dew-soaked grassy moat. Ethereal. The stuff of ballads, of fey folk and wandering maidens. A woman walks past, coaxing her dawdling, ancient terrier. A white van pulls up and the driver leans out to marvel at the scene. 'It's a gem,' he says. 'I've got a contract to clear the pavements around here. I can't believe my luck.' We talk about the approach, the priory ruins, the quaintness of the village. 'It's like stepping back in time,' he says. He waves me on my way, grinning broadly through his red beard.

He is right. Around the corner is the Nar Valley Way, open fields and mist, warmth settling, the thick smell of wet foliage. Another ballad moment: a setting for whistling wayfarers to wend their way, seeking fortunes, watching for riddling strangers at crossroads. A place for a young squire to walk, swinging a stick, dog at heels, pheasant in waiting.

It's a delight, this meadow-lush way, its expanse warrened with desire paths. And this is the problem. There are several possible footpaths, all poorly maintained, some designed and made by walking, others by the trampling of rushing wildlife and chasing dogs. Merrill's guide suggests a single clear path. Which is it? Mazy tunnels through the long grass peter out in untrimmed nettle and thistle. I lose half an hour of valuable footwork going back and forth, my trouser legs dew-soaked, my socks and trainers seeping. The sound of traffic steers me to a side road and I wade through knee-high tangle to reach it, skirting barbed wire and breaking through an uncut verge onto the tarmac, a wet, awkward birthing.

Nothing seems to match with Merrill here, either. Where to go? I need to get to Litcham, where I've agreed to meet my parents. There's that press of responsibility that comes with a rendezvous: I said I'd be there, so I have to be there. I can't spend the morning going round in circles, chasing the snaking tails of ill-trampled footpaths. I point myself towards the noise of cars to find the A1605 to Fakenham. I'll take the quiet back roads to Litcham. The Nar Valley Way looks good on paper, but if it's all this dense and unmaintained on the ground, I'd rather take my chances with farm traffic and speeding locals.

Aside from the odd passing car and a working quarry, the back lanes are quiet. A small black rabbit bounces in front of me and into a hedge. The sun is trying to break through, diffusing the cloudbank with sugary orange light. Am I on the right path? Who knows? I am not good at following directions, which is why this is not, I remind myself, a hiking holiday. I would not fare well on a walking tour: I'm too ready to be distracted, to follow curious byways, busy myself with hypotheses about abandoned buildings, be misled by pursuing a sound, a colour, a creature, a distant landmark. What's behind that hedge? What if I went that way instead? Is that a rock or a standing stone? Hopeless, butterfly sensibilities. Like Bunyan's hero, I give ear to the distractions of the world.

Does this make me an adventurer, or a wandering fool? I have a purpose, but this is not a quest. *There are many ways to Walsingham.* This is not about being exact. But, I remind myself, I have somewhere to be. I do need to get cracking.

Unlike Bunyan's Christian, my greatest adversity on this journey is a day's walking in wet socks. Following my nose instead of a map brings me to a farm and a charming row of sun-baked cottages, fronted with honeysuckle, clematis and hollyhocks. I have dry socks to change into when I stop. And I am walking into a landscape by Samuel Palmer, a track meandering uphill into a woodland pocket. I am here, and it is glorious. I am here. I am here. I am here.

Beyond the trees is a ploughed field, a raised ridge, a running hare. A bank of ox-eye daisies. A green 'stewardship margin' sign.

Sun and light rain together, walking the ruts of tractor tracks. It's so lost and arresting and unexpected here that I want to embrace it, to press my face into it, sink deep and wallow in it. I'm teetering between that longed-for state of immersion and the desire to possess: I want to bottle this moment and take it home.

Logistical concerns break the spell: the sign at a junction tells me I'm back on the Nar Valley Way, but so does a turning to the right. I think about joining up with Merrill's route, but I'm behind schedule now and it might take me a longer way than following the Lexham Road. I have a couple of signal bars on my phone, so send a message to my parents to let them know I'm running late. I break the rules to check online for the likely order of villages en route. I'm detouring wildly, but I will get there.

❖

A cluster of pebbledash cottages, an old covered buttermarket, a village sign at the crossways – East Lexham. This village is on Merrill's route, but I'm gaining it from the opposite direction. I'm walking contrary-wise as usual. The Saxon church tower appears above a flock of young, seemingly fresh-sheared sheep, black-footed and curious. A fingerpost sign at the junction states that it's only three miles back to Castle Acre by this road.

Church Farm: intricate chimneys cut with shortbread patterns. The call and answer of two chainsaws in the yard. Only three miles by road: I have faltered and meandered, frittering this chunk of the day away. No: I have dérived, drifted, not simply joined the dots with walking, and that's as it should be. And after all, what a morning! Now I just need to accept what goes with it – the extra time, the extra miles – and carry on.

Following the road through trees to Litcham feels like going downhill, a speeding up after the slow tangle of the journey's start. The Lexham Hall estate offers glimpses of white walls and windows between stately chestnut and oak, pastures of grazing sheep, brick bridges over running water. It's a scene dreamt by an Austen heroine, a Merchant Ivory arcadia.

An older couple on bicycles pedal towards me, the man behind barking at the woman in front: 'Keep in! Keep in!' She smiles, a distant grimace. Is this the pattern of their leisure time, or of their life together? It reminds me of the couple in the pub last night, a scene that I had pushed away and forgotten in sleep: the man lecturing about how to play a hand of cards, testing and hectoring, the woman flinching at every correction. I greet the cyclists as they draw near.

'Going far?' the man yells.

'Walsingham,' I say. He pedals on, giving no indication of

whether or not Walsingham constitutes 'far'. Perhaps it's another test, simply for the sake of testing.

❖

On the road into Litcham, a stall outside one of the houses is selling bunches of sweetpeas, with an honesty box. I cross the road to inhale the scent. A sign above the flowers apologises to honest customers for the need to install CCTV, due to repeated theft. Presumably someone is making off with the money box; do they steal the flowers too? I'd buy some to carry with me, but they would be crushed and shrivelled in a couple of hours.

The footpath parallel to the road runs behind a hedgerow, the air tunnel-damp and thick with blossom, wet earth and field stubble. As the road comes back into view, two coaches pass in convoy, both drivers smiling and waving. The heat begins to bloom.

I spot Dad's car parked by the road. Mum is in the passenger seat. She scowls when I wave and approach. It transpires that Dad has created a panic in the village: with no phone signal, he has fired wild rumours in the shop about my disappearance, asking for the use of a telephone, bemoaning my lack of response. The messages I sent on the way this morning, with updates on my progress, have not come through. I'm only half an hour later than

I expected to be, time spent retracing those winding missteps at Caste Acre.

In the shop, the women behind the counter know who I am, where I've been and where I'm heading. They laugh when I explain that I'm only slightly behind schedule and that Dad has been watching too many lurid true crime reconstructions on satellite TV.

'That's what fathers are for,' one of them says. 'Worrying.'

Mum is itching to leave after the long wait in the car, but I need to rehydrate and eat something. I switch to a daypack, change my socks and attempt to dry out my shoes in a patch of pavement sun while I breakfast on a cheese and onion roll, the only vegetarian fare to be had from the village shop.

'I've already walked over five miles,' I point out, petulant, sticking my feet out of the passenger door and spreading damp toes.

'And we've been waiting here since before nine,' Mum says.

Which explains it. I'd said to meet me at ten: that makes me an hour-and-a-half 'late'. No wonder Dad was about to call for a search party.

There was good reason, I recall, why I did this alone last time.

❖

From Litcham, Merrill's route takes the Nar Valley Way to Tittleshall. It seems a logical progression towards Fakenham, avoiding a swathe of main road, so we agree to follow it. The footpath runs alongside a field of pigs, their curved sties arks in a sea of mud. Walking past disturbs the pigs, whose movement disturbs the other residents: countless corvids, stalking for grubs, take wing together, a whole field-full lifting in one black, ragged mass. A single feather lands on the track in front of me. I pocket it for today's relic.

Beyond the pig farm, the footpath is in desperate need of maintenance, the grass almost waist-high in places. Mum likens it to walking in sand, the grass long enough to entangle the ankles. We wade on, reaching hidden cottages and signage worn thin by weather, following a combination of Merrill's directions, instinct and the shape of the land, to gain Tittleshall church. We pause on a block outside the church to stretch out our legs and rotate our ankles. After talking through the options, we decide to take our chances with the back roads towards Fakenham; abandoning Merrill to avoid further diversions, and picking up the A1605 for the inevitable final stretch.

Tittleshall to Fakenham is a psychogeographical survey of walking surfaces. The first stretch is newly tarred and chipped. The stones are sharp underfoot, the tar still unset treacle, but it encourages ownership, a pioneering stride and swagger and stamping-down. Further on, the smooth road surface is speedy as skating. The main road means revisiting the side-step jolts and irritations, the obstacle course of tangled verges, surfing against the blow of hot air with every passing truck. Freshly cut verges are dense, springy and soft: moon walking, ankle-twisting as trampolines. Despite the trudge, the A-road brings some delights: a pair of circling hawks; a Dutch gable farmhouse; two meadows carpeted with dog daisies and sprinkled with cornflowers. Wading birds with bright red legs – oystercatchers? – strut across a front garden and arrange themselves along the prow of bungalow roof, a mise en scène framed by Hitchcock. Truck drivers wave. I spot a giant plastic spider inverted on a path, legs clawing skywards.

We stop for a rest in the Fakenham garden centre café to refuel, where Dad meets us and worries about protein and hydration levels. The formica table top is cool to my wrists, the plastic chair a hard bucket to aching hips. Mum points out the tar stains that have worked their way from the new Tittleshall road surface into my cut-offs. She is bearing up well in her new walking shoes. After the last road stretch, we are both grimly determined.

It's getting close now. Expectation, and no small amount of adrenaline, fizz in my stomach as I alternate sips of tea and water. We calculate distances. Five miles from Castle Acre to Litcham. Two-and-a-half from Litcham to Tittleshall. Five-and-a-half to here. Another four to go. Dad drops us off beyond the roundabout and drives on to collect the keys from the shepherd's hut and await us at the Slipper Chapel. Mum and I brace ourselves for the final miles. As I roll from heel to toe at the roadside, waiting to cross, it finally sinks in: this time, I am actually going to make it.

❖

The last stretch to Houghton St Giles passes a Toad Hall, the East Barcham Arms and the grand East Barcham Manor. A man watering his garden just along the road offers us stories of the manor, the legend of Henry VIII walking from there to the Slipper Chapel, tales of a tunnel running through the chalk underneath, connecting to Binham Priory. A recusant access and escape route, perhaps. An old lady of the village, now dead, told of the sound of horses' hooves ringing against the hollow of the tunnel as they rode above it. 'The tunnel is supposed to go all the way to Cromer,' the man says, still watering the same fuchsia with his hose, 'although it's not proven. Except for the man with a dog who went down the tunnel at Binham and was never seen again.' Naturally, people said they could hear an unseen dog barking, lost in the tunnel or trapped by collapse. Or baying, but no longer living.

A kite circles on the rise. A footbridge over the ford, and here we are: The Slipper Chapel. Despite the mileage, this arrival feels sudden. Is it just too easy compared to last year? Do I deserve this place yet? Or can I simply not process where I am?

We wash our hands and faces with piped holy water from the push taps. The site is quiet, just the odd visitor reading information boards and pottering about. The shop and café have already closed, earlier than expected. Dad has acquired the key through a shuttling sequence of enquiry and negotiation, from Slipper Chapel to Shrine and back again. It would have been a very unhappy ending to have found myself sleeping on a bench tonight.

I go to put my backpack in the shepherd's hut. The sheep are in the field. The grey heron is guarding the water. The swans and mallards glide between reeds. It's all as before. There are some additional luxuries in the hut – an airer for clothes, a mug – but otherwise it's the same. I take off my shoes; hang out my socks and insoles to dry. Change into the otherwise unthinkable elegance of a skirt and flip-flops, in honour of a celebratory supper back at the East Barcham Arms.

It's not until later tonight, when I will sit alone in the hut on the edge of that narrow bed, watching the dark window, that it will finally sink in. It is nearly done. Tomorrow I will walk the holy mile to Little Walsingham, close the circle and earn my pilgrim's title.

❖

The still, morning car park suddenly fills with voices; a group disembarks from a coach and heads to the Slipper Chapel for Mass. There are two grey herons in the meadow this morning, guarding the reeds like bookends. The sky is a blue china plate. It's going to be a beautiful day.

My second entry to Walsingham will be via the holy mile. I need to do it this time, even if I do keep my shoes on. It's a narrow path with little verge, but it's early enough to avoid traffic.

This way into the village feels shorter than the old railway footpath, but maybe that's just walking with a whole foot, rather than a rotting one. The only passing car is driven by a nun, who grins and waves. I'm buoyed along today, speeding hungrily towards my goal, ready to soak myself in the stuff of it all. The Anglican Shrine is already teaming with visitors when I arrive: small clusters around guides giving tours and priests giving blessings. There's a private service in the chapel, so I wait it out at a café table in the grounds. The coffee is Church of England weak, guaranteed to provoke no carnal reaction, reminiscent of the Bovril-like cups I swallowed with my grandmothers in the church hall on Ely market days, visiting home from university. What would those women, both pragmatic chapel-goers, make of me sitting here, now? I feed toast crumbs to a blackbird who gets bolder by the minute, perching on the chair beside me, onyx eyes regarding me at a tilt.

In the chapel I write an intercession slip for Mum: I'm an interloper, but it's for insurance purposes. The inner Holy House chapel fills up with white-haired, wide-sandaled women who muscle me out of the space with tight smiles, arranging chairs around the edges and blocking off the tiers of votive candles. I take the hint, sit just outside and view the shrine through a window like a waitress hovering at a serving hatch. Just as the group's prayerful meditation begins, a shrine helper comes to top up the supplies for the sconces below the window, wheeling a creaky trolley and rattling hard handfuls of candles into the wooden boxes. This goes on for several minutes, despite turning heads and glares from the inner sanctum. I try very hard not to grin.

I eat lunch at the pub in the square, return for the afternoon sprinkling service and head back to the hut. I read pamphlets about asceticism and the giving of indulgences while supping a chilled tin of gin and tonic from the village store. I buy the kitschiest Our Lady T-shirt I can find in the shrine shop; walk to the church of Houghton St Giles in bare feet; paddle in the icy ford. In the evening, when the site is deserted, I weave a bouquet of grasses, feathers and wildflowers for the outdoor Madonna statue to hold, an antidote to the offerings of plastic posies and rosary beads. On the way back from brushing my teeth, I stop to light an overnight candle. Not only have I arrived, I have thoroughly settled in.

According to those stages of pilgrimage, I have arrived at the point of achievement, of consummation, my purpose realised. This is the moment of ritual fulfilment and intercession. I have walked my route; visited my holy sites; made my offerings. Now, I keep vigil over the field as night presses the window, hoping for a miraculous sighting of that running hare.

CODA

Homecoming

hymn

to the amorous graffiti of bus shelters   crouched in the shadows
of village bypasses

to the hieroglyphic cracks in their shatterproof panes

to the empty sockets of marble-raided cats'-eyes   leading to skid-
marks of make-shift shrines

to the calligraphy of their crimped tarmac treads

to the medieval fortress mazes of drain covers   sunk into swollen
cement

to their tangle-footed toe-tripping margins

THE FINAL STAGE OF PILGRIMAGE. Return. Reintegration. Facing the secular after a brush with the sacred. Fitting in again.

My parents arrive at the Slipper Chapel. We drive to the shrine office to return the hut key. Then it's a rapid unwinding of my route via the nexus of pilgrimage and transport routes: by car to Ely station, a train to London, another home, narrowly bypassing Canterbury. It takes a matter of hours to make the physical shift: a hut in a field next to a shrine; the sharp-elbowed swarm of bodies at Kings Cross. Walking the few metres from Kings Cross to St Pancras is stepping on a termite nest. The stress, the movement, the set expressions; forcing, pushing, scowling, nudging. No eye contact. No smiles.

I cannot escape permanently, but I can vow – and do, dodging the chicanery of wheelie cases – never to put myself through the wringer of daily commuting again.

On the train home, a suited young man hurls himself into the seat beside me, puffing, sighing, spreading himself out. Commandeering space. I turn to acknowledge him but he doesn't look at me once in the whole of his fifty-minute journey. Phone out, leg jogging up and down, flicking through a men's magazine. Sunglasses on. Earphones in. A force-field of not-noticing to enshroud and protect himself. But from what?

My note-taking suddenly feels like a pose, a fanciful,

eccentric habit from a forgotten time. I drink from a foldable water bottle instead of a takeaway coffee cup. My walking shoes are grubby. This time yesterday I was walking the holy mile with a stem of grass in my mouth, smiling at swifts. A hayseed. I stare out of the window and begin to fantasise about my next escape. Hell is a hurtling train carriage, packed with shutter-faced strangers, a perpetual surging and striving and forgetting to stop.

And this is it: my epiphany, the moment when I finally understand those medieval pilgrims who hazarded all to seek a place of sanctuary. The men and women who were fleeced or shipwrecked, who suffered injuries and injustices and could never be certain they would make it home. The penitents and the hopeful clutching their copies of *Informaycon for pylgrymes*, eking out their coins, sleeping in straw, haggling with hosts and guides. Why they returned, not to sit back and marvel at their achievement, but to begin once more the whole process of scrimping and saving, counting the months until they could afford to leave home and step out on the road, do it all over and over and over again.

This is the miraculous cure of pilgrimage – a shockwave through the futility of busyness.

❖

I have to go back to the Stone Chapel of Faversham, the eerie ruin among the crops that I discovered on the second day of my pilgrimage. It's a dare to myself as much as anything. Why be beaten by a place? Besides, there was more to my reluctance about stepping into that field than some irrational fear. It was a sense that I might disturb something at peace. It could be something beautiful, transcendent. It could be something wild and weird. Whatever it is, I must find it out.

Was I not looking for thin places, for moments of transport, for a peek behind the veil? This one is almost on my doorstep – a train ride and a short walk – and it's a disservice not to visit it again.

    It's the end of August and I have a meeting in Whitstable. Faversham is one stop away on the train, and it's the perfect time to strike out for the chapel, a short diversion on my way home. I have a notebook and pencil with me, and something else – a terrible trepidation. I feel as if I am carrying dread to this site. I want to tune in, but I'm afraid that anticipation might drown out all other senses.

❖

Leaving Faversham station, I think again of Arthur Machen, of *The White People*, of *The Great God Pan*, of the true sense of the word panic. I try to calm myself through noticing differences. The sun is high and hot: it is early afternoon on a Thursday, not a slow Sunday morning like my first encounter. The London Road is steady with traffic, a lorry or tractor for every few cars. It's a different time, if not a different place – so why not a different experience?

    Traffic. Dust. Barbecue smoke on a slight, warm breeze. A low garden wall, semi-dismantled. A dropped tobacco pouch. The resin-and-blackberry scent of a trimmed leylandii hedge.
Relax. Slow down. Be open.

Ospringe; playing fields; an orchard. Everything is a countdown to seeing that crop-field again, that copse of trees. Ripe, purple-black elderberries overhang the path, heavy with juice, bird droppings like smeared blood clots underfoot. Jazz and Dine at The Ship Inn. The Maison Dieu – a stone arch below, a bulging medieval barrel of a building straining at its timber struts above.

Chapel Car Sales is surely no coincidence. It's close. The fields are ploughed now. Across the stubble, a train snakes past and into the trees. The slow incline of the road is barely noticeable to the eye, but it adds reluctance to my steps. The tall bones of fennel, stalks sun-bleached, are skeletal in the hedgerow. Here's the false turning I took last time, before the Oare Road. Beyond the roundabout the rise is steeper, a crest beside Judds Folly Hotel, a sudden dipping down. This is the field then, opening to the right – do not look. Not yet. Eyes on the path. Follow the splintered line of tarmac. The bank rises to shield the right-hand view. I pause for a lorry to pass the narrow footpath, dry-mouthed.

A sudden lull in the traffic; the silence between waves; crickets.

The hedge falls away and there it is – a pile of stone low before the trees in a plain of shorn stubble. A swooping shot of rollercoaster adrenaline.

Hops are thick in the hedge. I stare at them to steady myself, edging forward. A sonorous shard of broken glass bounces against my shoe.

It looks smaller like this, the crop cut away, the structure evident at a distance. It looks like it should be quiet and cool, a place of respite in this broad August daylight. It should be less frightening, exposed rather than hidden, a secret laid bare. But it's a tiger in plain sight instead of crouching in the bushes. The flint teeth are visible from here, glinting in spikes of sunshine.

There's no getting around it. This place terrifies me.

But I keep going. Standing at the edge of the field, at the foot of the track to the chapel, every sound is splinter-sharp. Air stirring the clock-heads of brittle hawkweed. The whirr of a feeding dragonfly. A passing tractor-driver pips, jolting straight through me.

I have to do it. Push through the resistance, step over the cracked heads and bearded husks of crop leavings. Corn this year? Barley? The beards are too broken to decipher and I'm not stooping (taking my eye off the site, risking poor balance) to pick one up. The sun is a hot wall behind, my shadow squat in front.

With my first steps on the track there's a sudden, low groan, a sound from somewhere close. It's me. Ridiculous! I keep going and the ground bears me forwards, falling away like the bottom of a swimming pool, rolling me towards those ragged walls.

Somehow, here I am. The stones almost touchable, paces away; the bonding courses of thin Roman brick clearly visible, running through the walls like terracotta striations in rock. Not yet. I slow things down by reading the small English Heritage information board, keep it, a shield, between me and the structure.

Can I go in? My ankles are sinking again. It's like looking at a ferocious beast through the bars of a cage. Why get too close? Do I dare myself to touch? It's possible to walk the perimeter. I do, testing the edges like palpitating the extremities of a wound, keeping my feet close to the strimmed crop margin. The copse is shady. Someone has stopped here for a beer. But the postholes in the chancel wall are staring sockets and the tree limbs creak above as I pass, pause, test my will.

At the far side of the site, the walls recede from view. The relief is like the loosening of a bandage. A train shouts in the distance. There are no birds. A pair of blue, torn, men's underpants hang on the stubble edge. Another beer bottle – this has been a camp for someone braver, or more foolish, than me.

I make it all the way round the perimeter, back to the information board, and stare at what must have been the opening. Can I step into the mouth? I must try. Low nettles guard the entrance, a stinging welcome mat. Not this way. I move along, dare myself to touch the hot flints of a jutting block of fallen wall. There's a gap here, wide enough to step through.

No. It's okay; I am in one piece. But I'm still not going in.

Walking away, the ground springs up to meet me, will me on. Do I feel watched as I leave? Yes. Do I look back to check? No. The contents of my backpack shift and slosh like an unsettled stomach, a watery-bowelled fear.

I wait until I reach the roadside to look again. A single pigeon swoops the field, rises over the chapel's tree-roof and keeps going. I don't blame it. I won't take away a relic of this place today, in case, like a trinket in a story by M.R. James, it summons something up.

I stumble back along the London Road: lightheaded, pulse hard in the wrists. Arms heavy. The reassurance of residential streets call to me: Victorian terraces far from the ancient footfalls of Watling Street; hollyhocks and hibiscus; children on scooters eking out the last school-free days; cats basking in windows; dogs and shopping bags.

By the time I get home, my body has all the symptoms of shock. Chill. Exhaustion. Emotional drainage. I feel like I need to be sick. I feel like I need brandy, a blanket and an early night.

The Stone Chapel is definitely a thin place. Sacred

through centuries: use, neglect and reuse spiralling around. I feel a presence there, but of what, I'm not sure. Is this place just a marker of age and ancient sorrows, of the mourners who buried their dead there, or the pilgrims desperate for cures? Or did something terrible happen in the copse, staining the site? Do those walls contain a memory of violence or despair? Am I feeling a lived fear, years or generations or centuries after the act? I could dig through archives, maybe unearth a trauma, but I don't want to know. It is enough to have felt the ground grab my ankles, and pull myself away.

ACKNOWLEDGMENTS

I have many to thank for making this book possible. Thank you to my editor Tom Chivers for his faith in the idea, and to all at Penned in the Margins. Thank you to those who provided succour of various kinds, including Canterbury Christ Church University for early stage financial support, Mark Hall for sharing his research, and the many helpful folk I encountered on the road. A debt of gratitude to my dear rescuers and provisioners on the way: Rosie Coupe and her partner Michael Hessey; my parents Terry and Shirley Overall. Thanks to my friend and colleague Peggy Riley for keeping me on track and offering a fellow writer's encouragement. Most of all, thank you to my husband James Frost, and son Rowan Frost, for supporting what became one of my most eccentric walking whims.

SOME SOURCES

Anderson, William. 'Blessing the Fields? A Study of Late-medieval Ampullae from England and Wales.' *Medieval Archaeology*, 54:1, 2010, 182-203.

Bondeson, Jan. *A Cabinet of Medical Curiosities*. I B Tauris, 1998.

Bunyan, John. *A Pilgrim's Progress* [1678]. Project Gutenberg online.

Burgess, Anthony. *A Dead Man in Deptford*. Vintage, 1994.

Chaucer, Geoffrey. *The Canterbury Tales* [<1400]. Librarius dual text online.

Dean, Dinah. 'The Legend of the Miraculous Cross of Waltham'. Waltham Abbey Historical Society, 2002.

Debord, Guy. 'Theory of the Dérive' [1959]. *Situationist International Anthology*. Edited and translated by Ken Knabb, Bureau of Public Secrets, 2006, 62-66.

Duffy, Eamon. *The Stripping of the Altars*. Yale, 1992.

English Heritage. www.english-heritage.org.uk

Ewan, Ruth. *No Tail*. Strood, 22nd December 2015.

Hall, Mark A. 'More Feet Washing.' *Peregrinations: Journal of Medieval Art and Architecture*, 2:3, 2009, 178-9.

- 'Research Query: Pilgrims' Footbaths?' *Peregrinations: Journal of Medieval Art and Architecture*, 2:2, 2007, 1-2.

Hasted, Edward. 'Parishes: Tong.' *The History and Topographical Survey of the County of Kent: Volume 6*. W Bristow, 1798, 132-143.

Harpur, James. *The Pilgrim Journey*. Lion, 2016.

Heywood, John. *The play called the foure PP* [c.1544]. The Hieronimo Project online.

Historic England. www.historicengland.org.uk

Holy and Healing Wells. www.insearchofholywellsandhealingsprings.com

Hunt, James. *The life and extraordinary adventures of Sir William Courtenay, knight of Malta* [1838]. https://archive.org/details/lifeextraordinar00cantrich/page/n0

Johnson, B.S. *Albert Angelo* [1964]. B.S. Johnson Omnibus, Picador, 2004.

Lambarde, William. *A perambulation of Kent* [1576]. https://archive.org/details/perambulationofk00lambuoft

Koenig, John. *Dictionary of Obscure Sorrows.*
www.dictionaryofobscuresorrows.com

Machen, Arthur. 'N' [1936]. Tartarus Press, 2010.

- *The Great God Pan* [1894]. Dover, 2006.

- *The White People* [1904]. Penguin, 2012.

Mapping Chaucer. mediakron.bc.edu/mappingchaucer

Merill, Rev. John. www.johnmerrillwalkguides.co.uk

Nunn, Rev. Andrew. Southwark Cathedral Visitor's Guide, 2018.

Ohler, Norbert. *The Medieval Traveller.* Boydell, 1989.

Rochester Bridge Trust. www.rbt.org.uk

Royal Herbert Pavilions. www.royalherbert.co.uk.

Sebald, W.G. The Rings of Saturn. Vintage, 1999.

Wells, Emma J. 'Making 'Sense' of the Pilgrimage Experience of the Medieval Church.' *Peregrinations: Journal of Medieval Art and Architecture* 3:2, 2011, 112-146.

memoriam   for visible roadkill

anisoptera
bombus
columba livia domestica
columba palumbus
erinaceus europaeus
oryctolagus cuniculus
passer domesticus
phasianus colchinus
vespula vulgaris
vulpes vulpes

two dragonflies, one bumblebee, several feral pigeons, two wood pigeons, two hedgehogs, three rabbits, several house sparrows, one pheasant, countless wasps, three foxes, and doubtless many others unseen, RIP